FROM GUILT TO GRACE

Dwight Carlson, M.D.

HARVEST HOUSE PUBLISHERS
Eugene, Oregon 97402

To Betty,
my cherished best friend,
companion, counselor,
sweetheart, and wife.

FROM GUILT TO GRACE

Library of Congress Catalog Card Number 83-080118
ISBN 0-89081-375-2

PREFACE

Almost certainly the greatest problem plaguing mankind is guilt and shame. Its influence is widespread and its effects on all of our lives is staggering. It is felt not only by people with emotional, spiritual, or physical problems but by every "normal" person as well.

This book explores the subject of guilt—what it is, how it develops, and its devastating and diversified manifestations. We will look at why religion, including Christianity, adds its load of guilt. The formative role of parents and society will also be examined.

We will then suggest specific practical steps that you can take to combat guilt in your life. We will conclude by helping you appreciate God's solution to guilt—His grace! The goal of this book is to help you get a grasp on the phenomenal forgiveness, freedom, joy, and peace that God desires for all of His children.

Examples in this book are true, but incidental features have been changed to protect identities.

I greatly appreciate the tremendous assistance in typing and editing given by my wife, Betty, and my niece, Lyn Carlson.

CONTENTS

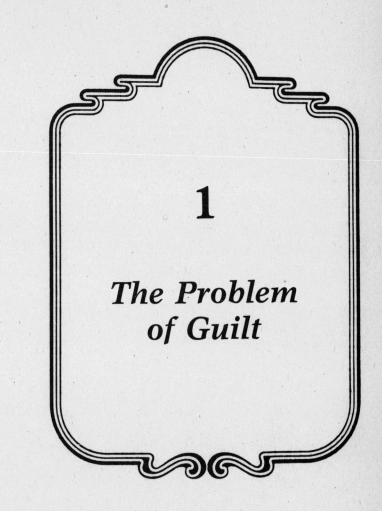

1

The Problem of Guilt

I was ready to see my next patient, Jeri. She stormed through the door, marched across the room in a very deliberate fashion, stood over my desk, and started tearing up a green piece of paper.

"What's she tearing up?" I wondered. Then in amazement I realized that it was money. Was it a one-dollar bill, a ten, a twenty, or a fifty? Then I caught a glimpse of one of the pieces as it fluttered down on my desk. I realized in horror that it was a hundred-dollar bill! When she finally finished tearing it up, she breathed a sigh of relief and said, "There, I feel better now." We talked about it for awhile, and then I asked, "What do you want me to do with this pile of money?"

"Just throw it away—*just throw it away,*" she said.

So I put it in my basket along with the rest of my trash, and we went on with our session.

You see, Jeri was being plagued by a guilty conscience because she hadn't declared all her waitressing tips. And she desperately wanted to rid herself of this guilt.

Then there was Tim. Tim was a 19-year-old

whom I saw in the emergency room. He was dragged in by the police in handcuffs, crying out, ''Let me out of here! Let me out of here! I want to kill myself!''

As I talked with Tim, I could almost feel the guilt oozing from him. ''You know, I've broken people's arms,'' he said. ''Unless I'm high on drugs, I just feel so guilty, and I can't get rid of it. I just want to die—please let me die, let me kill myself.''

Tim was a drug-pusher, and if people failed to pay, he would literally break their arms. A few years before he had had a big argument with his dad, and he had stormed out of the house. That same night his dad was rushed to the hospital, where he died of a heart attack. Tim has been blaming himself ever since for his dad's death.

Guilt, guilt, guilt! It's all around us—it's everywhere. You may be thinking that these are extreme and interesting cases from a psychiatrist's notebook, and that they certainly don't happen to ''normal '' people. You may feel you can't relate to guilt so intense that it causes a person to tear up a hundred-dollar bill or to want to commit suicide.

But all of us wrestle with guilt in some way almost every day. What young person hasn't felt guilty over cheating on a test, smoking pot, or going too far with the opposite sex? Then there are the white lies—what you were doing last night, who you were with, or why you couldn't go to the in-laws on Sunday. Or what about using the copier at work for your personal duplicating, exaggerating on your income tax, or padding your expense account?

But even if you work hard to avoid these areas of guilt, there still arises the guilt created by other people's demands—the demands of society, parents, children, friends, God, or your own strict conscience. Everything is an "ought," a "should," or a "must." Life is a demand, not a gift. God is a harsh taskmaster, a celestial kill-joy instead of a loving Father.

It's these everyday pressures that mount up to create tremendous guilt in individuals' lives. These pressures rob people of their joy and happiness, and when they accumulate they can lead to serious physical, emotional, and spiritual problems.

Let's take a look at Marge, for example. Marge may live next door to you or work at the desk next to yours. The only thing that seems to be wrong with Marge is that she complains occasionally about her nagging health problems. She's had several problems, including headaches, spastic colitis, heart palpitations, and numbness. She's been from one doctor to another, and though they do all kinds of tests, they find nothing.

Marge has a very strict religious background. Not only was she brought up in very rigid parochial schools, but she was raised by a mother who was harsh and emotionally cold. As an adolescent, Marge rebelled by being sexually promiscuous. Confession brought no relief from the guilt, and years later she still seems to be doing permanent penance. She finds it very hard to enjoy anything. When things go well she feels uneasy, thinking it's "the calm before the storm." She tells herself, "You don't deserve this."

Or consider Bob and Christy. They have been married for eight years and are chronically fighting. They aren't aware of any obvious guilt, but as you dig underneath their chronic marital turmoil you find that Christy had an affair two years into the marriage. She's never told anyone and has almost forgotten it, but it continues to extract its toll.

And Bob? He's trying to go up the corporate ladder, and he's working long, hard hours. He's out of town a lot and feels guilty about that. Each partner is unconsciously expressing his guilt by attacking his spouse over various incidental issues, thereby keeping the marriage in constant discord.

Or there's Jack, a conscientious young Christian. He is somewhat compulsive and is striving for perfection in order to be accepted by his family and God. In his continual effort to please God he has increased his giving to the church until he is giving 30 percent of his meager income.

A major cause of Jack's problems is unresolved guilt. When he was 15 he discovered what masturbation was all about, and he has been plagued with guilt ever since. When he was 17, Jack talked with his minister, hoping to get some relief. Instead he was told, "Well, yes, it is a sin—after all, that's what the monkeys do." And so Jack left his minister's study weighed down with more guilt.

Some people who have a problem with guilt don't even know it. Robert, age 22, is a case in point. He complains of back pain so hasn't worked much in his life. For years Robert has stifled his feelings, including a lot of accumulated guilt. And no doubt this is the cause of his back pains.

As we look into his past, we see an extremely harsh, inconsistent father who would unmercifully beat Robert with a three-inch wide belt. If he cried, he would just get spanked more. So he learned to swallow his tears and all the accompanying feelings.

His mother, on the other hand, would try to protect Robert by lying for him—but if the truth ever came out he would get double punishment.

So Robert's models were a harsh, inconsistent father and a lying, protective mother, who also stifled his feelings. When he would come running to her after his father had beaten him, crying, "I hate Daddy—I hate him," what was her response? "You shouldn't feel that way—after all, he's your father."

In order to relieve his own guilt, Robert's father would buy his son many things, including a series of new cars when he was a teenager. All these things served to confuse Robert as his character was forming, making it difficult for him to know right from wrong, when to listen to feelings, and how to express his feelings appropriately.

As you can see from these examples, guilt is everywhere. Over the years I've come to the conclusion that guilt is the number one problem plaguing mankind. It robs us of the freedom, peace, and joy that God has intended for His children. His truth and grace are meant to free us, not to leave us in bondage to our failures and guilt.

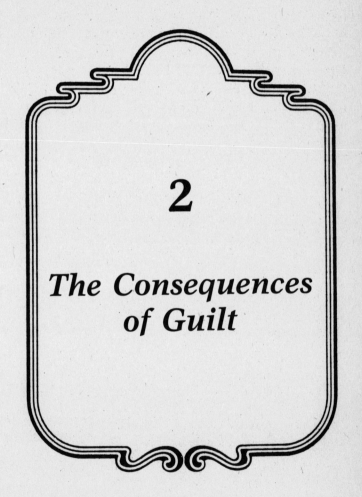

2

The Consequences of Guilt

A letter addressed to "Uncle Sam" said, "My doggone conscience has been working on me, so to shut it up, I'm sending you this money order for $400." It was signed, "One of your conscience-stricken nephews." A postscript was added, saying, "P.S.: If I still feel guilty, I'll send in the other $400."

It all started in 1811 when someone sent five dollars to the United States Treasury Department with the anonymous note, "I defrauded the U.S. government. Here is some money to pay it back."

The government, not knowing what to do with that five-dollar bill, created the Conscience Fund. To date that fund has received about five million dollars. All kinds of notes and amounts of money have come in. Sometimes the people sign their names and sometimes they don't. Others, for fear that the government will catch up with them, send their letters through a priest or a lawyer.

One frequent conscience-easer is the check for 15 or 20 cents—payment for a reused postage stamp. (The postage stamp wasn't canceled so the person peeled it off and used it again.) Many people do this with hardly a qualm while others feel extremely guilty about it.

Then there was the check sent from an ex-I.R.S. employee—one dollar for four ball-point pens—and the person who anonymously sends two cents in an envelope every 90 days, no one is quite sure what for.

Some people carry their guilt for years, as in the case of the man who recently owned up to wartime atrocities committed 30 years earlier, and the World War Two veteran who attached this note to his Conscience Fund contribution: "While I was in the Air Force, I took a few things that did not belong to me. I am now a Christian and would like to make it right."

Guilt was eating away at these people, and only confessing many years later afforded any relief. The author of an article on the Conscience Fund wrote, "Born-again Christians have become a godsend to the treasury. A large percentage of those with conscience fund contributions credit a religious conversion for prompting their payment" (*Los Angeles Times,* Nov. 19, 1981).

A more drastic consequence of guilt is apparent in the Guyana tragedy. In the aftermath of that tragedy one survivor said of Jim Jones, "He kept them working because they thought if they went against him, they were going against God." So many people in these extremist movements are brainwashed into thinking that if they go against their leader they're going against God. They think that whatever their leader says is straight from the Almighty, so even if he orders them to commit suicide, they do it.

Anytime there is an infamous murder many innocent people "confess" to the crime. At least five such people confessed to being the Los Angeles "Hillside Strangler." These are individuals with a tremendous amount of guilt who are looking for some way to salve their conscience.

Psychiatrist Theodore Reik wrote in 1925, "Guilt cries out to be punished, and the confession partly satisfied that need. The unconscious need for self-punishment has to be considered one of the most important emotional forces shaping the destiny of man." And the guilt may be so intense that it drives the person to self-destruction.

So guilt can cause extreme behaviors. But it also causes more common, everyday reactions. Guilt has something in common with an itch. Both are feelings that annoy us, so that we would rather convert the annoyance to something else, even if that "something else" is pain. Dermatologists can tell you of people who will scratch an itch until it bleeds rather than endure that itch.

Guilt is the same way. No one likes that gnawing discomfort that says, "You're wrong, you've blown it again. See what you did?" Guilt always carries with it that awful feeling that "I'm to blame." So we convert to something else, to other kinds of symptoms that are more psychologically or socially acceptable. *The Comprehensive Textbook of Psychiatry* says, "The feeling of guilt appears almost universally in definitive depression, and the anticipation of this feeling—that is, potential *guilt—plays a part in almost every mental illness."*

Guilt is often linked with depression, but it can also cause anxiety, sexual problems, obsessive-compulsive behavior, aggressiveness, fault-finding, criticism, denial, and manic behavior. It can cause behavioral problems, alcoholism, and Type A (driven) behavior. It also causes psychosomatic symptoms of all kinds, chronic pain symptoms, and dermatological manifestations. In fact almost any physical symptom can be related to guilt.

Because it is such an uncomfortable emotion, guilt gets distorted into these other forms, which then removes the person one step further from the true problem. Often the sufferer tries to treat only the symptoms without curing the primary problem. From a psychiatrist's or a physicians's point of view, it is harder to deal with the guilt because it is camouflaged.

But guilt can have more subtle, everyday manifestations. Few people would ever suspect that aggressiveness can result from unresolved guilt. It's somewhat like the old adage, "The best defense if a good offense." So these individuals are aggressive in interpersonal relationships, on the road or in the courts. They may be very "successful" in life, but usually at the expense of other people.

Anger and guilt are often closely related. The aggressive person attacks other people in order to protect or defend against his own deep feelings of guilt. Often these guilt feelings are totally unconscious. Nevertheless, his hostile attacks lead to more guilt. Thus it's often true that guilt leads to anger and anger leads to guilt.

Guilt is often the driving force behind the workaholic. He works hard to win approval—to show that he is worthwhile. Often the aggressive individual and the workaholic have a great need to succeed. They have to prove to themselves and the world that they have nothing to be ashamed of.

There is a flip side of needing to succeed to compensate for guilt. Some people will unconsciously not allow themselves to succeed because they feel they don't have the right to succeed—they feel they are flawed and guilty. About the time they are ready for a promotion at work, for example, they mess up.

I found it interesting to learn that there is a group that helps people cope with the "problem" of wealth. I don't know about you, but I wouldn't mind being stricken with that affliction! Apparently, however, some people find it to be a problem. A *Los Angeles Times* article (Sept. 23, 1978) said: "When Robert Martin suddenly received a gift of a million dollars, it was an event that brought no joy into his life. Instead of pleasure and freedom, his newly acquired wealth was accompanied by feelings of guilt, fear and embarrassment, all of which contributed to years of serious emotional turmoil."

Another subtle expression of guilt is feeling inadequate or having poor self-esteem. More precisely, these feelings are due to shame, which is closely related to guilt. When we do not think well of ourselves we have deep-seated feelings of being ashamed of ourselves.

When you stop and think about it, right in the beginning of the Bible are the first classic examples of the consequences of shame and guilt. The story of the first sin in the Garden of Eden is inevitably followed by the first encounter with guilt. Genesis 3:6-13 says, ''When the woman saw that the tree was good for food, and that it was a delight to the eyes, and that the tree was desirable to make one wise, she took from its fruits and ate; and she gave also to her husband with her, and he ate. Then the eyes of both of them were opened, and they knew that they were naked; and they sewed fig leaves together and made themselves loin coverings. And they heard the sound of the Lord God walking in the garden in the cool of the day, and the man and his wife hid themselves from the presence of the Lord God among the trees in the garden.'' Note that they hid from God. That is an important point. Guilt always makes us hide from ourselves, other people, and God.

''Then the Lord God called to the man and said to him, 'Where are you?' And he said, 'I heard the sound of Thee in the garden, and I was afraid because I was naked, so I hid myself.' '' Here we see guilt caused shame and fear.

''And He said, 'Who told you that you were naked? Have you eaten from the tree of which I commanded you not to eat?' And the man said, ' The woman whom Thou gavest to be with me, she gave me from the tree, and I ate.' Then the Lord God said to the woman, 'What is this that you have done?' And she said, 'The serpent deceived me, and I ate.' " Thus Adam and Eve lied, blamed others, and attacked others for their sin.

Two things resulted from eating the forbidden fruit: a series of *feelings* followed by a series of *behaviors.* What were the feelings? Guilt, fear, anxiety, and shame—all resulting from just one sin.

The series of behaviors were the following: They hid, lied, blamed, attacked, and covered up.

Then, a few verses later, we read: "And the Lord God made garments of skin for Adam and his wife, and clothed them." God erased their guilt with a proper covering and sacrifice. He actively stepped in to free them from guilt. Here we see the first instance of sin and guilt. We also get a glimpse of God's overwhelming grace.

You only have to turn the page to see the next encounter with guilt, in the story of Cain and Abel: Abel's offering to God was accepted; Cain's was not. This resulted in feelings of guilt, inadequacy, and jealousy. God offered Cain the opportunity to make amends by making the correct offering. Instead, Cain yielded to his aggressive and vengeful feelings, and murdered his brother. This, in turn, caused further guilt, alienation, and loneliness (Genesis 4:1-16).

The account of Joseph illustrates how enduring an entity guilt is, and how it can crop up many years later. You remember how Joseph was sold by his brothers into slavery in Egypt (Genesis 37). Many years later, when Joseph was a ruler in Egypt, his brothers came to him to buy grain to survive the famine in their land. Joseph didn't reveal himself to his brothers immediately. Repeatedly, when things went wrong the brothers were guilt-stricken. Even on one occasion when things went unexpectedly well, their guilt feelings surfaced (Genesis 42, 43).

This is what happens to us too. We can go along for years, but unless we've adequately dealt with our guilt, that old problem may pop up unbidden and plague us. Often in my office patients bring up guilt feelings regarding incidents that happened 20 or 30 years earlier.

Guilt feelings inevitably cause destructive emotions and behaviors, which often become self-destructive. As we saw illustrated in Genesis, the feelings are not only those of guilt and shame, but also those of fear, anxiety, jealousy, inadequacy, and anger. That's what goes on inside us, often automatically and without our even being aware of the cause. Frequently this leads to destructive, self-defeating behavior: blaming, anger, attacking, aggressiveness, criticizing. It can also lead to hiding and paralysis, causing a person to be inactive, not wanting to do anything at all. The person who is the victim of repeated criticism soon feels that no matter what he does, it's wrong. "I can't do anything right," he feels. Pretty soon he says, "If I can't do anything right, I won't do anything at all."

THE SNOWBALLING EFFECT OF GUILT

Over the years guilt can start building up, and for many people it becomes unbearable. Going back to the dermatological example, suppose I have a little rash and it itches, so I start scratching. Do you know what happens? It feels a little better. But then what happens? As soon as the tissue begins to heal, it itches again. And if I'm prone to this condition, I'll start scratching again. This in known by dermatologists as the scratch-itch-scratch cycle, and the condition can spread all over the body.

Unfortunately, that's what sometimes happens with guilt—there's a snowballing effect. Let's say that someone feels guilt because he didn't succeed in his parents' eyes—he didn't get good enough grades and didn't accomplish enough—and his parents said, "Oh, you'll never amount to anything." So young Joe sets out to prove that he's going to amount to something. He tries to make a million or two million dollars—it's a common story—and he becomes a workaholic. But what is the consequence of being a workaholic? More guilt, because Joe is probably not spending enough time with his family. If he tries to solve his guilt problem by working harder, it just creates more guilt, until the whole thing becomes a vicious cycle.

Or take the person who is aggressive and blames other people. If this person feels guilty over something, instead of dealing with it honestly (which requires a great deal of maturity) he blames other people instead. And the fallout of blaming other people is simply more guilt.

Then there's the person whose guilt causes him to withdraw into inactivity, into virtual paralysis. He is doing less and less at work and is terrified that he's going to be found out. And the more fearful he is, the more he shuts himself into his room in the office. His guilt and fear cause paralysis or procrastination, which then causes even more guilt.

Here's a common one—the Christian who feels anxiety. Some dear brother or sister in Christ quotes Philippians 4:6 to him: "Be anxious for nothing." So what happens? Now he has guilt on top of his anxiety. I've seen people like this struggle for years, barely holding themselves together. Then some desperate morning they call me, though they're terrified about getting psychological help. Why? Because "good Christians shouldn't need that!"

These are some of the ways that people get into a tailspin with guilt, a tailspin which can plummet them into severe depression and even suicide.

Another thing which adds to the snowballing effect of guilt is that the person who feels guilty is often the one who is more sensitive to guilt in the first place. He goes through life wearing rose-colored glasses, and everything he sees is tinged with guilt. What these people have to ask themselves is, "Am I too sensitive? Is it all coming from me? Am I wearing rose-colored glasses?"

Then there are some people who never feel guilty. What they have to ask themselves is whether they're callous to guilt, whether they're failing to sense it, whether they're numb to their emotions.

One last consequence of guilt: Our unresolved guilt and our sensitivity to guilt can even affect our reading of the Scriptures and our view of God. The person who is troubled with seeing guilt in everything may even have a hard time listening to a sermon, even if it's not an especially guilt-inducing one. Recently I had a patient who was seriously threatening to kill herself. She had just heard a Sunday morning message with a few too many "shoulds," and it was too much for her.

When I was between the ages of 17 and 23, some people in a certain Christian group were very influential in my life. I learned some good things and maybe got a few hang-ups. One of the things that we were encouraged to do was memorize verses, and over the years I memorized several thousand. Recently I've gone back and reviewed them, and I was struck with how many of the verses had "shoulds," "oughts," and warnings of all kinds. Not many were about God's love, grace, and forgiveness. I was viewing the Scriptures through those guilt-tinged, rose-colored glasses. I know those verses were helpful in many ways, but the selection left me with a harsh God and a lot of guilt.

The point is that when we read the Scriptures or listen to a sermon, how we feel affects how we view what we read or hear. Someone who is really depressed can only see the harsh aspect of God's commands and judgment. Paul Tournier in his book *Guilt and Grace* says:

> Our complexes influence us even in reading the Bible, when we seek in it inspiration for a line of conduct which is freer and more in conformity with the will of God. It is like what happens with the three-dimensional cinema where the spectator, in order to obtain a stereoscopic vision, wears glasses of two colours so that each eye sees only one part of the projected image. Thus, each one of us sees in the Bible what corresponds to his preconceived ideas and his complexes. . . . Thus we constantly risk being influenced by our psychological make-up in our interpretation of the Bible (pp. 46-47).

It is pivotal to realize that all of these consequences and problems with guilt occur whether the guilt is valid or not valid. The most insidious thing about guilt for the sincere Christian is that its results are equally devastating whether we are actually guilty or whether we just think we are.

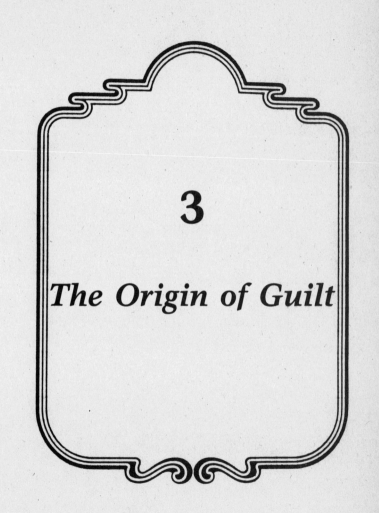

3

The Origin of Guilt

I was only 19 years old, and I thought I was going blind. My eyes were burning terribly, and when I checked them in the mirror I saw that the pupils were dilated and the whites were beet-red. But worse than the pain was the paralyzing fear that God was punishing me by striking me blind.

And why would God be punishing me, you might ask? Because I had just seen my first movie, and I was convinced that movies were sinful.

The background to this scenario is as follows: I was in the Navy, stationed near San Francisco, and my duty that night was to usher at the base theater. Coincidentally, my eyes had been dilated by an ophthalmologist that same day, but they seemed fine when I reported for duty. I could have stayed in the foyer during the movie, but I decided to yield to temptation and see what these movies were all about. And so I went in.

In actuality, all that happened was that my eyes had been strained by watching a movie when they were dilated. But I thought God was striking me blind.

This incident describes the dilemma of guilt

for all of us. Imprinted on my mind was the belief that seeing movies was wrong. I don't remember my parents or the church saying it was wrong, but still I "knew" it was wrong. And violating that belief brought about intense guilt feelings.

People react to this story in two different ways. Some can clearly identify with what I was going through; others think my reaction was just silly.

Those who can't identify with it have a different background from mine, and it sounds ridiculous to them to give a second thought to seeing a movie. But those who grew up in a fairly rigid religious background can identify with this story—those who grew up in the days when lipstick, movies, dances, and just about everything else was "sinful."

The original source of our beliefs is our conscience, a God-given entity which serves as a regulating agency to bring us to God, to teach us right from wrong, and to give a degree of stability to society. I believe that within the conscience is a basic core which all of us have, something that gives us universal standards of right and wrong. Over the years, layer upon layer is added to this core as we accumulate more standards of right and wrong.

Cultures that are totally isolated from one another still have some common beliefs and rules, and if they violate them, they feel shame or guilt. All of mankind believes in some sort of higher power. Virtually all societies feel ashamed if they don't cover their nakedness. Most cultures believe that murder is wrong and adhere to many of the other Ten Commandments.

So there are certain basic laws that God has instilled in all of our consciences, and about which we all tend to feel guilty. Freud even agreed in the inherited nature of conscience; it is not solely the result of early childhood influences. Psychiatrist Carl Jung referred to it as the "collective unconscious."

The Book of Romans states that certain standards are inbred in men: "For when Gentiles who do not have the Law do instinctively the things of the Law, these, not having the Law, are a law to themselves, in that they show the work of the Law written in their hearts, their conscience bearing witness, and their thoughts alternately accusing or else defending them" (Romans 2:14,15). Psalm 36:1 reiterates this thought: "Transgression speaks to the ungodly within his heart." This embryonic conscience is very susceptible to molding by our early environment. At birth we are uncivilized, undisciplined, self-centered, and very needy individuals. Nothing is expected of us; all of our needs are met. But before long, expectations arise. The child meets with disapproval when he cries at the wrong times, like three in the morning when mother's tired and dad won't get up. Before long that little baby gets the feeling that this is right and that is wrong, and perhaps even senses that when he does what's right he gets love, and if he doesn't he gets a frown or is left alone. Before long these approval/disapproval messages become internalized. That is, the baby accepts the messages as part of his own belief system.

Just last week I saw a vivid example of this process. I was in a parking lot, and in the car next to me was a mother and her preschooler. The little girl had gotten some cookie crumbs all over the back seat of the car. In disgust the mother said, ''You're good for nothing.'' To this the girl voluntarily responded, ''I'm good for nothing.'' The way this was said by the child suggested that the message was well on its way to being internalized.

I once did age-regressive hypnosis with a patient, and she was able to remember an incident that happened when she was 18 months old. She was in a playpen when her relatives visited, and she remembered putting out her arms to her uncle. He started to pick her up, but then suddenly set her down. The relatives laughed, and even at that early age she was able to sense rejection. You see, she had dirty diapers. This was the first in a series of events in her life that left her with the feeling of shame. Without her even realizing it, the message ''We don't approve of you'' was being imprinted on her mind.

Another patient recalled that when she was only three years old she didn't want to go out and play with her friends, an unusual behavior for a child. As best we could trace it back, her mother always wanted her to be perfectly groomed and dressed. So even at age three she can remember thinking, "I'd better not go out and play because I might get my dress dirty." To this day she won't open her front door unless she is immaculately groomed, or else she feels extremely uncomfortable—a discomfort that is the result of submerged shame and guilt.

These early imprints can affect us many years later. A woman in her sixties came to me because of marital and sexual problems. As we went back in her life, she recalled an incident that she had forgotten for many years. When she was five years old she was behind a bush with yellow flowers "comparing genitals" with a little boy. She remembered her mother finding and scolding her, and the accompanying deep shame. The memory gave insight into some of her present inhibitions, but another interesting fact was uncovered—she understood why she has always loathed the color yellow. Yellow was forever linked in her unconscious mind with that yellow-flowered bush and the tremendous shame she felt.

So we can see how young minds are affected and molded, and if we violate what has been conveyed to us in the past, we feel tremendous guilt, often without understanding its real basis. Soon we learn that you should do this, you shouldn't do that, boys don't cry, big boys and girls don't wet the bed or throw food on the floor. There are a thousand and one injunctions—do this, don't do that. Just think of all the injunctions planted in the mind on the subject of dress alone! You could probably come up with about a hundred rules, such as not wearing stripes with a plaid, or a tie with a T-shirt, or unmatched socks, et cetera.

The development of our conscience, and ultimately our beliefs, can be compared to the crafting of a key. The ridges on the key have to be just the right height for the corresponding pins in the lock, or else the lock won't open. If the ridges are either too high or too low, the key won't work.

So it is with our conscience. In order for us to be in God's will, free of guilt and experiencing the peace of God, the configurations of our conscience must be crafted according to God's ideal plan.

Figure 1 illustrates God's ideal for us. If our beliefs were exactly what God would have them be, our belief system would have this configuration:

Figure 1: God's Ideal

God's Ideal: _____

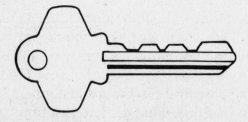

When we're born, our conscience consists only of deep instinctive leanings, just like the key in Figure 2, with a very basic outline of what God would have in our life:

Figure 2: At Birth
God's Ideal: . . . .

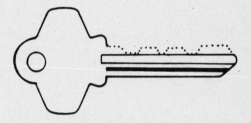

If our parents or our society have somewhat loose morals, we might be taught that their values are the right "key" (Figure 3):

Figure 3: Lax Parents / Society
God's Ideal: . . . .
Actually Taught: _____

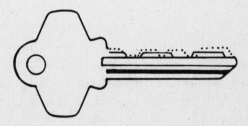

Our parents might say, "Forget God; just love your neighbor—if it doesn't put you out too much." But there still remains a portion of God's universal laws deeply ingrained within us which will tug away at us later.

Other people have learned a lot of do's and don't's from very rigid parents or backgrounds, and they have a belief system that looks like Figure 4:

Figure 4: Rigid Parents / Society
God's Ideal: . . . .
Actually Taught: _____

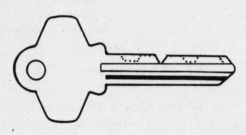

The theory is that the more standards you have and the higher they are, the better. But what happens when you make your standards too demanding? Soon you become overwhelmed with all that is required of you, and this virtually guarantees that you will foul up.

I think Satan's preferred strategy is to keep the standards too low. But his second choice is to make the standards too strict. The person who conscientiously tries to keep the impossibly high standards soon gets so bogged down in life that he loses his whole sense of God's grace. He often becomes depressed or develops other symptoms, whether physical, emotional, or spiritual. What Satan doesn't want is for us to find the right configuration—God's ideal standard.

Noted ethnologist Konrad Lorenz discovered in the late 1930s that if he took a goose away from its mother as soon as it was born and had a cat or a human being serve as the mother instead, the goose would follow its surrogate mother around just like it would have followed a mother goose. At a certain critical age very early in its life, the goose would imprint that surrogate mother in its mind and thereafter would think of that animal as a friendly animal even though that animal might in fact be a natural enemy.

That's precisely what happens to us. We're imprinted with the do's and the don't's and the shoulds and the oughts and the musts that the important people in our life convey to us very early in our experience. This happens without our even realizing that it is taking place.

What we don't realize is that from birth onward there is a "tape recorder" inside our heads, reeling away silently. It is recording all these rules, whether they are valid or not. Then for the rest of our lives, when something triggers that tape recorder, it plays back the appropriate tape for the situation. Suppose you have the "I must be perfect" tape in your head. All it takes is one stimulus, such as forgetting to send your grandmother a birthday card, and the tape plays, tormenting you with guilt over your failure— you're only 99 percent perfect. Without our realizing it, these tapes play away, either goading us into action or censuring our wrong behavior. They are responsible for a great deal of the conflict and irrational behavior in our lives.

Proverbs 22:6 emphasizes how important our early training is: "Train up a child in the way he should go; even when he is old he will not depart from it." God is saying that it is a parent's responsibility to train a child properly, to imprint the right things upon him that he will follow later.

Unfortunately, we can imprint the right or the wrong things. We can imprint positive or negative things; we can send mixed, conflicting messages, or ones impossible to attain.

It is interesting to note that the word "ought" and the word "owe" come from the same root. So often when we feel we ought to do something, we feel we owe it, as if it is a debt to be paid.

Psychoanalyst Karen Horney wrote (*Neurosis and Human Growth,* 1950) that external expectations and demands frequently become a "dictatorial tyranny." These become internalized as rigid dictates that manifest themselves as shoulds, oughts, and musts. They often become coercive, causing us to be hypercritical of ourselves and other people. Hypersensitivity to the perceived judgment and criticisms of other people is the natural result of these stringent inner demands.

In order to measure up to these standards (which our parents or other important people often didn't realize they were imposing upon us) we try harder and harder to meet them. If we don't go that route, we rebel and throw everything overboard, with guilt as the inevitable consequence.

There's also the problem of the inconsistent parent. A good example is Robert, who was referred to earlier. With a harsh father and a lying, protective mother, it was very difficult for him to establish standards of right and wrong.

A good Scriptural example of the inconsistent parent is Rebekah, who urged Jacob, her favorite son, to lie to his father in order to cheat his older brother of his birthright. As we see in Genesis 27, Jacob had qualms about lying, but Rebekah told him, "My son, only obey my voice." And so Jacob was in a no-win situation—if he disobeyed his mother he would feel guilty, but if he obeyed her he would be deceitful to his father.

That's precisely the bind in which many of us have been placed in the past—one in which we simply can't win. It doesn't even have to be a father versus a mother; sometimes just one person can put us in a no-win situation. The old adage "Do what I say, not what I do" puts us in that bind. The model tells us to do one thing, but the actions tell us to do something else. Even worse dilemmas occur when another person imposes his will upon us, telling us that we do not have the right to feel what we in fact are feeling.

These things affect all of us as we grow up, and we later have to wrestle with them to try to figure out what is right and wrong for us personally. The more we are aware of the development of guilt, the better equipped we are to combat inappropriate guilt.

THE NATURE OF GUILT

In order to understand the nature of guilt, a few terms need defining. Sin is transgression of law. Guilt results from having committed a breach of conduct, particularly by violating a specific law, while shame is more a generalized feeling of "I just don't measure up" or "I'm a failure!" Shame has more to do with the idea of being ashamed of myself as a total person, being disgraced, whereas guilt comes about as the result of a specific action or behavior.

Conscience comes from two words, "to know" and "guilt"—in other words, "to know if I'm guilty." Our conscience judges us according to our belief system, and our belief system primarily comes from the basic template that God has put in our hearts and from the important people or influences in our life, whoever and whatever they might be. Guilt feelings are the normal response to any violation of our internalized belief system.

We all know what guilt feels like—it is that uncomfortable gnawing sense of "I shouldn't have done that." These feelings can be exaggerated, denied, distorted, or converted to other symptoms.

The crucial thing to realize is that guilt can be based on valid or *true beliefs,* which I refer to as *true guilt* or *true guilt feelings.* I believe that the ultimate basis for true beliefs is the Word of God. True guilt is the result of breaking God's absolute rules.

The diagram below illustrates true guilt. When valid beliefs are violated it causes guilt.

True Guilt:

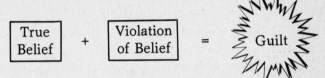

In contrast is *false guilt*. This is the result of beliefs that we cling to but which simply aren't valid. It may be the belief that I'm dumb, no good, or ugly, or that I have to be perfect. But if I believe any of these, I'm going to react as if it were actually true. This is often referred to as *neurotic guilt*. The formula for false guilt is: invalid beliefs that I cling to as valid and which result in guilt when violated.

False Guilt:

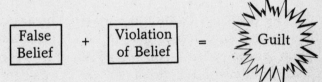

The guilt feelings are just the same and equally devastating as if they were based on valid beliefs.

A couple of other terms need defining. *Displaced guilt* is when we feel guilty in one area of our life, but actually the guilt is related to some other area.

Another type of guilt is *free-floating guilt,* in which we feel vaguely guilty but we don't know why.

Then there is *unresolved guilt,* or the *unresolved guilt fund,* which is comprised of all of the unresolved guilts in our past. This is very similar to the unresolved anger fund discussed in my book *Overcoming Hurts and Anger* (Harvest House Publishers, 1981).

I believe that any of these unpleasant emotions such as hurt, anger, or guilt that we don't deal with appropriately can be buried, creating terrible problems for us later in life. If we don't deal with guilt it can create turmoil, depression, and psychosomatic problems, stealing away the joy that the Lord intends for us.

WHEN GUILT STRIKES

Why does a government employee steal four ball-point pens costing a total of 60 cents, then endure the agony of guilt for years, and finally send a dollar to the Conscience Fund?

It might be a little easier to understand if we consider an unmarried, pregnant 16-year-old who is wrestling with what to do with that pregnancy. She didn't plan to get pregnant during that evening of pleasure, but now she is struggling with the consequences of her action.

First let's clarify the relationship of both pleasant and unpleasant feelings relative to guilt. Guilt primarily strikes after we've done an act which is contrary to what we believe is appropriate. On the other hand, while we are contemplating or engaging in the act in question, it often seems pleasurable, or at least seems the easiest course of action to take at the time. Thus the 16-year-old girl is pressured by her boyfriend, and she doesn't want to lose him. He says that if she really loves him she will engage in sex. In addition she has her own needs for affection. Thus she yields, either not thinking of the consequences or negating the possibility at the time. Only later is she hit with the reality of her impregnation and the guilt and dilemma of what to do about it.

A look at the graph on the next page illustrates this phenomenon. "Time" is represented on the horizontal axis, with "feelings" on the vertical axis. As we have said, during the act itself pleasurable feelings dominate. But after the act the unpleasant ones take over. In our example, the unmarried 16-year-old is engaged in heavy petting leading to intercourse. Pleasant feelings predominate until the evening is over, when feelings of guilt ensue. These unpleasant feelings persist for long periods of time, depending on each specific situation.

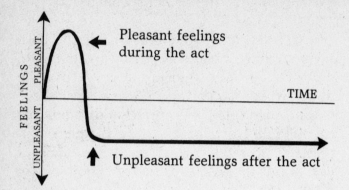

Several conclusions can be drawn from this: 1) Guilt generally strikes after an illicit act. An awareness of this can help us to consider an act more seriously before impulsively yielding to temptation. Freud referred to this phenomenon as the Pleasure Principle versus the Reality Principle. 2) The total amount of unpleasant feelings far surpasses the total amount of pleasant feelings when we violate God's laws. 3) Guilt often remains for extended periods of time, and, like the "itch," people will do almost anything to get rid of it. The government employee who stole a few ball-point pens will after years of gnawing guilt send in a dollar to the Conscience Fund to relieve that guilt. No wonder Mark Twain's Huck Finn said, "Conscience takes up more than all the rest of a person's insides"!

4

Guilt Trips

One day I received an unusual gift in the mail—a postage stamp. It was sent by a charitable organization, and was accompanied by the following letter: "Dear Friend: I have taken money from the blind to entrust you with this valuable postage stamp. You can use it for many good things: to pay a bill, mail a birthday card, or to write to an old friend.

"Or, you can use it—and I hope you will—to send a tax-deductible gift to_____, the only worldwide Christian medical mission to the blind.

"I know this about you, that you are someone who cares, someone who acts on what you believe...."

A line further down said, "You and I have never met, yet I'm willing to trust you, sight unseen, with this postage stamp, the potential future of one blind child."

It closed with "God bless you" and a not-so-subtle P.S.: "Treatment costs us about $14.30 per patient; $100 treats seven."

An envelope was enclosed with a blank place for that stamp, and a commitment card to fill out. The question was: What should I do with this letter and unused postage stamp?

This type of guilt trip happens all the time in our society. You are given a token gift, but it ties you all up inside because you have to decide how to extricate yourself from the bind in which you've been placed—totally against your will. You can feel guilty or angry, or you can throw the letter in the wastebasket, but even then it may still bother you. And so there's almost no way to win with this kind of "gift."

When I was chairman of our church, I somehow got placed on a mailing list for Christian leaders. A magazine was sent to me with an advertisement for a do-it-yourself kit for creating fund-raising letters. Here's the formula:

1. Tell the story of an actual individual. Establish geography, sex, age, and so on. This is the secret of successful fund-raising.
2. Tell an incident that illustrates the subject and the need.
3. Tell how the problem could be solved, leaving the "if" factor dangling.
4. Show how your organization can come to the rescue.
5. Universalize.
6. Tell how the contributor can have a share in this great work.
7. Build in a hook. This can be an irresistible offer, a wonderful premium, or an appeal to the emotions.
8. Give exact instructions.
9. Flatter your donor.
10. Add a P.S. which repeats the instructions and the irresistible offer.

The organization that dreamed up this do-it-yourself kit for mass-producing guilt (in my opinion) works with numerous well-known Christian evangelical and world relief organizations.

An article in the *Los Angeles Times* (Nov. 25, 1982) quoted a consultant to Christian organizations as saying, "Many donors react emotionally to appeals, 'giving when the emotional jolt exceeds a certain level.' " The article cited an actual example of this emotional shock treatment, used in a letter pleading for funds for starving children: "By the time you read this, this child will probably be dead."

These things grieve me because of the toll they take on people's lives—people who later come to my office for help. The sensitive person can become inundated, either responding in knee-jerk fashion to the emotional pleas or else feeling guilty if he doesn't. Other people become callous and indifferent even when responding would be appropriate for them. In the long run everyone loses.

But in the short run guilt trips are very effective for those who exploit them. The postage stamp method of persuasion will probably net a great deal of money. However, in the long run it has horribly devastating cumulative effects on the recipient, and sometimes a backlash effect on the originator of the guilt trip as well.

Before we look at the types of guilt trips, let's examine God's purpose for guilt. There is a positive purpose for this much-maligned entity, despite all the negative things we have been saying about it so far in this book.

GOD'S PURPOSE FOR GUILT

God's purpose for guilt is to bring us to a right relationship with Him, to give some moral stability to society, and to guide us in appropriately respecting the rights of other people.

John 16:8 shows how God uses true guilt feelings, initiated by the Holy Spirit, to draw people to God: "And He, when He comes, will convict the world concerning sin, and righteousness, and judgment." An example of true guilt is given in 2 Samuel 24:10: "Now David's heart troubled him after he had numbered the people. So David said to the Lord, 'I have sinned greatly in what I have done. But now, O Lord, please take away the iniquity of Thy servant, for I have acted very foolishly.' "

Another way God uses true guilt is to alert us to the fact that we have violated a relationship with another human being. For example, 1 Corinthians relates that a member of the church was committing incest, and the church was doing nothing about it. Paul wrote and told them to do something about it—not to just let it go. After the church corrected the situation Paul wrote again, saying, "I now rejoice, not that you were made sorrowful, but that you were made sorrowful to the point of repentance; for you were made sorrowful according to the will of God, in order that you might not suffer loss in anything through us."

He concludes, "For the sorrow that is according to the will of God produces a repentance without regret, leading to salvation; but the sorrow of the world produces death" (2 Corinthians 7:9,10).

God uses this sorrow or these true guilt feelings to alert us to the fact that some corrective action is necessary on our part to restore our relationship with God or our fellowman.

SATAN'S MISUSE OF GUILT

But anything that God *uses* Satan will *abuse*. The word "Satan" means "adversary," and Satan can clearly be seen in that role in the book of Job.

Another meaning of the word "Satan" is "accuser." We see him in this role accusing God's people both in Job and Zechariah (Job 1:6-11; Zechariah 3:1,2). The word "devil" is a Greek word meaning "slanderer" or "false accuser." Revelation 12:10 calls Satan "the accuser of our brethren. . . who accuses them before our God day and night." Satan continually works at creating and causing guilt in sincere Christians— it is one of his choice methods.

First Peter 5:8 warns, "Be on the alert. Your adversary, the devil, prowls about like a roaring lion, seeking someone to devour." Ephesians 6:11 says, "Stand firm against the schemes of the devil." Second Corinthians 2:11 adds, ". . . for we are not ignorant of his schemes." Satan abuses guilt and beats us over the head with it. If we're going to be joyous Christians, we must be aware of his devices.

Four of the most common misuses of guilt are the following:

1. Guilt trips—using guilt to manipulate people.
2. Hypersensitivity—making us too sensitive to guilt.
3. Adding to what is written—adding to the rules that God has given us in Scripture.
4. Accusations—lying and distorting the truth.

GUILT TRIPS

While working on this manuscript, I was interrupted by the doorbell. A boy was at the door. He handed me a newspaper, asking if I would like a complimentary copy. Of course I said yes and took the paper from him. He proceeded to tell me about the virtues of the newspaper and his need for three more subscriptions so he could win a trip to Catalina Island. At the end of his speech I politely told him I wasn't interested in subscribing to the paper. His curt response? "Then why did you take the copy I gave you?" This is a classic example of the *Obligation Guilt Trip*.

TYPES OF GUILT TRIPS

Guilt trips fall into several recognizable categories. The first is the *Obligation Guilt Trip*, illustrated at the beginning of this chapter with the "free" postage stamp and the "complimentary" newspaper just described.

In each instance, a token gift is given to obligate the recipient, and thus causes guilt if he doesn't respond. The political field is well aware of the effects of obligatory guilt trips; this is precisely why politicians aren't allowed to accept gifts (sometimes referred to as bribes)—their voting may be influenced.

The Bible illustrates this principle in Joshua 9, describing an enemy nation giving gifts to the Israelites. This resulted in an ill-advised covenant, which caused later tragedy to Israel.

A "letter to the editor" graphically illustrates how requests for contributions obligate the recipient. This letter was written by a senior citizen on a fixed income, which limited how much he could give away. He wrote, "I feel compelled to send money I need to pay bills, because I have been trapped, embarrassed and manipulated by the implication that I would 'rob' the needy if I didn't 'fork over' " (*Los Angeles Times,* Dec. 18, 1982).

Another type of guilt trip is the *It Will Be Your Fault* variety. An example is the teenager's statement to his mother: "If you don't let me use the car tonight I won't be able to study with Joe, and if I get a bad grade on the exam tomorrow it will be your fault." A stronger statement used on one of my patients is: "If you don't loan me the car tonight I'll steal one, and if I'm caught it will be your fault."

Next we come to the *Shame on You* guilt trip:

"If you don't give me money to get the car fixed, I'll have to walk four miles to work. It might even rain—how could you make me do that when you're my own flesh and blood?" This seems almost laughable when you see it in print, but this kind of guilt trip extracts tremendous tolls from people like you and me every day.

There are several *Shame on You* guilt trips recorded in the Bible. David's older brother, Eliab, was a soldier in the Israelite army, which was cowering from Goliath. David was told by his father to bring food to his brothers at the front line. When he heard Goliath's threats, he innocently asked his brother why no one had tried to fight Goliath. When Eliab heard this, his "anger burned against David and he said, 'Why have you come down? And with whom have you left those few sheep in the wilderness? I know your insolence and the wickedness of your heart; for you have come down in order to see the battle' " (1 Samuel 17:28). This is a perfect example of the *Shame on You* guilt trip. "Shame on you for leaving your sheep," Eliab is saying. Note also that Eliab's accusation stemmed from his own guilt, because he was one of the Israelites who was afraid to fight the giant.

David provides a good example of how not to buy into this guilt trip: "But David said, 'What have I done now? Was it not just a question?' then he turned away from him." David verbally rejected the guilt trip and turned his back on it— an effective strategy.

There's another *Shame on You* guilt trip in Mark 14. After Mary had anointed the feet of Jesus with costly perfume, the Bible says, "Some were indignantly remarking to one another, 'For what purpose has this perfume been wasted? For this perfume might have been sold. . .and the money given to the poor.' And they were scolding her" (verses 4,5).

In John 12 we find that one of those self-righteous individuals was Judas, "who was intending to betray" Jesus. Just like David's older brother, Judas's accusations sprang from his own guilt. The *Shame on You* guilt trip is typically judgmental, striking at a vulnerable spot with us, which we all have. Often we start those self-incriminating tapes playing in our minds: "You're spoiled, you're selfish, you're not spiritual enough, you're not dependable."

Then there's the *Threat of Being Exposed* guilt trip. An example is this 22-year-old daughter's statement to her mother: "If you don't give me some money for new clothes, I'll come to your aunt's wedding in my jeans." The mother doesn't want her daughter to show up at the wedding in jeans, so she forks over the money. "I'll expose you—I'll make you look bad" is the message.

I think that asking people to come to the altar to show their dedication to God can have elements of this kind of guilt. I've attended Christian banquets where there has been this kind of exposure pressure. All who want to contribute "x" amount of dollars are asked to raise their hands. Those who don't are exposed.

Next we have the *Laying on the Guilt* guilt trip. This is something that is valid in and of itself, but when used excessively to hammer home a point it becomes destructive. It's like using a big club: "Your aunt will be disappointed if you don't go to her birthday party. You know she has heart problems and she might have chest pains if you don't come. And after all your uncle has done for you over the years. . ." And on and on it goes. They're all valid points, but when the person starts laying it on thick, the valid points are changed into guilt-laden ones. I remember going to religious meetings as a boy and singing eight to ten stanzas of "Just As I Am" while patiently waiting for someone to respond to the altar call. I recall one service where we kept singing stanza after stanza, but no one responded. Finally one man came down the aisle, so the minister justified the waiting by saying, "See, we waited all this time just for this one soul." Yes, one soul may have been saved, but think of the scores of souls who have been turned off from Christianity by these techniques.

Motivation by Guilt

Motivation by guilt is a powerful club. Both the church and the world use this club to further their own purposes. The world uses sex as a motivator, and parades it all over your television set, enticing you into buying the sexy car or the sensual perfume. The world also has what 1 John 2:16 calls "the pride of life"—status symbols that appeal to our pride, in the never-ending race to keep up with the Joneses. Power, money, influence, and possessions are more of the world's manipulators.

The church can't use these motivators, since they are so blatantly crass. So the church is left with guilt and manipulation. The catch is that when prompted by the Holy Spirit, there *is* a place for true guilt in the church. However, there is a line that is easily crossed when the church resorts to the misuse of guilt.

It isn't only religious organizations that use guilt to motivate. Many secular groups are fueled by guilt, from the PTA president pressuring a mother to bake cookies to the neighbor begging you to collect signatures for a petition.

The Bible tells us to be aware of the tactics that are used against us, to be as "wise as serpents" (Matthew 10:16 KJV). We need to be sensitive to God's prompting and to the legitimate needs of the world, and yet not be motivated by misused guilt or manipulative methods.

People use guilt trips for various reasons—for power, for manipulation, and for personal gain. Sometimes they use guilt trips because they have unresolved guilt in their own lives, so they only know how to operate on the plane of guilt. Unfortunately, I believe many Christian leaders operate on that plane. They may be involved in the cause of the church or organization because of their own guilt, and they haven't risen above that level. They feel they "must" serve or "should" help, so that is what they tell other people also.

When I was on the pastor-seeking committee for my church, I listened to scores of sermon tapes of excellent ministers. Some messages contained powerful guilt trips. I can't help but wonder if some of these men hadn't fully realized God's grace in their own lives.

Unless we have experienced the grace of God and seen the freedom we have in Him, we live under guilt, and we're going to communicate that same standard to the people around us. This happens at all levels, not just from minister to congregation, but from one Christian to another. If a person is guilt-motivated, that's all he can pass on to other people. And that's tragic.

Motivation by Love

I believe that most of us are drawn to God by the vehicle of true guilt. Through the prompting of the Holy Spirit we are convicted of our sin and our need for God, and so we come to Him. But as we grow as Christians and begin to realize God's phenomenal grace in our daily lives, our response to Him should be more and more one of love and gratitude, and not one of guilt.

God desires a relationship of love, not one of guilt, duty, or legalism. In the Old and New Testaments, God says repeatedly that it is not sacrifices He wants but that we know and love Him. In Hosea 6:6,11 (TLB) God says, "I don't want your sacrifices—I want your love; I don't want your offerings—I want you to know me.... I wanted so much to bless you!" (See also Micah 6:1-8.)

When Jesus asked Peter to feed His lambs, meaning God's children, what was the motivating statement? Did He say, "Peter, if you feel guilty, feed my sheep"? Did He say, "Peter, if you see all the needs of the world, feed my sheep" or "Don't you realize they'll all go to hell if you don't bring them into the kingdom"? No! Jesus simply asked, "Peter, do you love me?" (John 21:15-17). Then He said, "If you love me, feed my sheep." That's precisely the relationship He wants with us. As we experience His love and grace, we will go beyond a guilt motivation to motivation out of true love.

5

More Is Better?

*T*he minister I was listening to said, "You can always do more!" In my younger years I took statements like that very literally. Thus I adopted a very harsh God who had me driving myself in an effort to please Him. But at some point you can't drive yourself much further, and I was near that point.

You see, the Model T spark coil that I had hooked up across the foot of my bed to wake me up couldn't jolt me out of bed anymore.

As a teenager I had gone through some lean years spiritually. Then at about 17 years of age I committed my life to the Lord, and wanted only to please and serve Him. After high school I felt the Lord calling me to work in a Christian servicemen's center near a large Marine base. So I moved there on my own, living in a trailer and supporting myself as a mason's tender. Every spare minute I spent at the servicemen's center, sharing Christ with Marines who were heading for the battlefields of Korea. Since my quiet time alone with God was important, I set aside an hour every morning for this. Witnessing was also very important, so I logged the number of times I talked with other people about Christ each week, and on and on it went.

Needless to say, I was driving myself. I would get to bed at 11 or 12 P.M. night after night, and then that alarm clock would go off at 5:30 in the morning. I got to the point where I just couldn't go on any longer, and I had to back off from it all.

HYPERSENSITIVITY

This is typical of many Christians who are striving, honestly and sincerely, to please God and to find answers to their lives. People come into my office who are spending three hours a day studying the Bible, trying to solve their spiritual and emotional problems. I see others who are giving 30 percent of their income to the Lord's work, also in an effort to resolve their conflicts. These kinds of activities, when driven by a hypersensitive conscience and carried to an extreme, can make Christianity extremely burdensome.

No wonder the *Comprehensive Textbook of Psychiatry*, Volume III, Page 3200, says, "Religion provides mechanisms both for intensifying guilt and alleviating it." In my opinion that statement is right on target.

Paul Tournier, a Christian psychiatrist, says in his book *Guilt and Grace*, "I cannot study this very serious problem of guilt with you without raising the very obvious and tragic fact that religion—my own as well as that of all believers—can crush instead of liberate" (page 23).

Guilt is often something inflicted on us by

other people, as in the case of guilt trips or Satan's accusations. But more often than not *we* are the ones who ultimately inflict the most guilt on ourselves. Then, in order to alleviate this guilt, we drive ourselves even harder, until the situation becomes virtually masochistic.

Masochism generally refers to sexual perversion, characterized by pleasure in being abused. It also means pleasure in being abused or dominated by another person, and is often used to mean self-abuse or hurting oneself. Freud felt that masochism was influenced by guilt. What happens is the people who feel guilty (at either a conscious or an unconscious level) may punish themselves in an effort to free themselves of their guilt.

Societies in the past and even some in the present practice masochism. Some went so far as to offer their children as sacrifices to the gods. The cry of the heart is, "God, I will give You my very best—then won't I be free of guilt?" In the Old Testament, Baal's prophets committed masochistic acts: "So they cried with a loud voice and cut themselves according to their custom with swords and lances until the blood gushed out on them" (1 Kings 18:28). They were desperately attempting to get the attention of their gods.

Masochism wasn't solely an Old Testament phenomenon; a subtle form had crept into the New Testament church too. Look at Colossians 2:14,16,18: Christ has "canceled out the certificate of debt consisting of decrees against us and which was hostile to us; and He has taken it out of the way, having nailed it to the cross. . . . Therefore let no one act as your judge in regard to food or drink or in respect to a festival or a new moon or a Sabbath day. . . . Let no one keep defrauding you of your prize by delighting in self-abasement." Through Christ we have the free gift of grace—a tremendous prize—and Paul is saying that we shouldn't let anyone take that away from us. In these Biblical instances masochism is used in the sense of *asceticism*—punishing the body by self-abasement or depriving oneself of pleasures. By and large, the modern-day church does not practice masochism in the same ways as then (fasting, forbidding marriage, or wearing somber clothing). However, there are more subtle forms: the demands and shoulds that are placed on us.

These are the issues over which I wrestled for many years. As a young Christian I was urged to memorize three verses a week, a habit that proved to be of tremendous help to me. I thought, however, that if three was good, six must be better, so I memorized six a week. Then I felt guilty when I couldn't remember the ones I had memorized eight weeks before.

Or take the matter of having a quiet time. If 20 minutes a day was good, 30 minutes must be better; and if 30 minutes was good—and on and on it went, until I needed the Model T coil to get me out of bed in the morning. As I look back on my life, I can certainly see elements of masochism.

During this same period in my life I joined the Navy, and saw people "requisition" (a euphemism for stealing) government property. It was clear to me that I shouldn't steal—not even a pen or paper clip. One day I quickly needed to address an envelope so I grabbed the closest writing instrument—a "U.S. Government" pen. After mailing the letter my hypersensitive conscience struck me with the nagging question, "Did I steal U.S. Government ink?" My assumption was that the more sensitive I was, the better.

During those years I was not aware of any external forces pressuring me to do more. But now when I hear such statements as, "If you are not tithing, tithe; and if you are tithing, give more," or, "Does your heart have room for one more child?" I can see how they subtly imply, "You aren't doing enough" and "More is better." It doesn't take much emphasis on this philosophy to create tremendous loads on the sensitive, conscientious person.

There is another variety of modern-day masochism—the belief that we have no rights. Some people teach that we as Christians have absolutely no rights—we are to be totally unselfish and perpetually giving. The basis for this belief is Christ's command to go the second mile if someone asks you to go one mile with him, and to turn the other cheek if someone slaps you (Matthew 5). In other words, you must surrender your rights to anybody at any time. I maintain that if you really believe this to the nth degree, you have no right to own a home, to own a second set of clothes (and maybe not even the first set), and to have a bank account. Why? Because you have no rights, and someone else needs your house, clothes, and money.

Just this week a friend told me about a Christian speaker who said, "May all we do be for others and for God, not for ourselves." If you were to take this literally, you would never brush your teeth. You would never pour yourself a bowl of cereal in the morning, because it isn't directly serving God or other people. These are extreme examples, but this kind of thinking trips up many people in ways that are much more subtle. Some would feel guilty leaving their children with a sitter in order to make shopping a little less of a hassle. Or they would feel guilty buying an outfit that is a little more expensive than usual, or for taking a week's vacation just to do "nothing."

Nevertheless, we must be *willing* to give up all of these items and "rights" to God, just as Abraham was willing to offer his son, Isaac, to God (Genesis 22). God may challenge us on things we grasp too tightly, but to say we have no rights whatsoever is inconsistent with the real world in which you and I live.

One last word about "more is better." Even if you're a paragon of dedication, sincerity, spirituality, perfection, and efficiency, you can always do more. Consequently this philosophy leads you to view your accomplishments as being of little or no value. This is precisely where Satan would have us be. If he can't tempt us with overt sinful pleasure, he'll sidetrack us with more subtle means. We can eventually fall by sheer exhaustion, then break under the load. It may take longer with this method, but the results are equally satisfying to the enemy.

Thus, *more is not better!* We should strive to be sensitive to God's wishes, while being careful of the pitfalls of hypersensitivity.

ADDING TO WHAT IS WRITTEN

"Where then is the sense of blessing you had?" This is the question that Paul asked the Christians at Galatia, and it is a question that could be asked of most people who have been Christians for awhile (Galatians 4:15). What has happened to the joy you felt when you first became a Christian? What has happened to your "first love"? (Revelation 2:4).

Mathematically, the simplest way to increase guilt is to increase the number of beliefs, which inevitably will increase the number of violations. The phenomenon of adding to what is written, adding rules that are not in the Bible, spans recorded history from the Garden of Eden up to the modern-day church.

Old Testament Examples

Genesis 2:16,17 (TLB) reads, "But the Lord God gave the man this warning: 'You may eat any fruit in the garden except fruit from the Tree of Conscience—for its fruit will open your eyes to make you aware of right and wrong, good and bad. If you eat its fruit, you will be doomed to die.' "

One day Satan, "the craftiest of all the creatures," approached Eve and said, "Indeed, has God said, 'You shall not eat from any tree of the garden'?" He raised the big question, "Did God really say that?" Eve added to what God said by saying, "You shall not eat from it *or touch it*, lest you die." God had just said not to eat it, and she added *"or touch it"* (Genesis 2:17; 3:1,3).

Now we might say that this is a very small difference, but picture this scenario: Imagine Satan giving Eve a real sales pitch about the desirability of the fruit from the Tree of Conscience. Then Eve misquotes God, saying that we shouldn't eat it or touch it. Satan then touches a piece of fruit and says, "Look—I didn't die." Then he picks a piece and touches Eve on the arm with it and says, "See, you didn't die either." She hasn't done anything wrong yet, but Satan has already made her violate what she believes to be God's law. This greases the skids for the next crucial step—violating God's law.

I've seen people get into trouble because wearing lipstick or not going to church is as bad as illicit sex to them. By adding to God's laws, many people violate the essential commands of God.

In 1 Samuel 13 Saul had just disobeyed God's commandment by offering a sacrifice, a priestly function that the prophet Samuel was to conduct. Thus Saul was truly guilty. He then went out to fight the Philistines, and commanded that no one was to eat that day until they had defeated the Philistines. That sounds very virtuous, since fasting was a common practice of the day; however, this day they were going into battle and needed energy. Saul's son Jonathan didn't hear the command because he was already in battle. While he was fighting he became weak from hunger. Finding some honey, he ate it, "and his eyes brightened." Later he was informed of his father's edict. His response? "My father has troubled the land." In other words, Saul was making unreasonable demands on a tired army (1 Samuel 14:24-29).

The rest of the Israelites didn't eat that honey, which was perfect food for the situation. But do you know what they did later? They butchered some animals, and because they were so hungry they failed to drain the blood the way they were supposed to, according to God's commandment.

This is an important point to realize. Every time we make an addition to one of God's commands, we increase the likelihood of breaking His actual commandments. We can only keep so many, and that's why we need to keep the ones actually written in God's Word.

New Testament Examples

The Pharisees were famous for loading people with excessive demands. Jesus said, "You would think these Jewish leaders and these Pharisees were Moses, the way they keep making up so many laws! And of course you should obey their every whim! . . . They load you with impossible demands that they themselves don't even try to keep" (Matthew 23:2-4 TLB). The Pharisees, quite literally, added to what was written. The Old Testament law as given by God had 613 commands. Trying to be helpful, the Pharisees elaborated on these, adding hundreds more.

Take, for example, the single command to keep the Sabbath day holy. They managed to make 39 laws which amplified that one command alone! That is why Christ said of the Pharisees in Mark 7:9, "You nicely set aside the commandment of God in order to keep your tradition." In Mark 2:27 Christ focused on the real meaning of the Sabbath: "The Sabbath was made for man, and not man for the Sabbath." They had missed the heart of God's intention and command regarding the Sabbath.

Consider the command to tithe. Jesus said to the Pharisees, "You tithe down to the last mint leaf in your garden, but ignore the important things—justice and mercy and faith" (Matthew 23:23 TLB). God had told them to tithe, and being such literalists they didn't know where to draw the line. If they had ten mint leaves in their garden, they would give one to God. Jesus told them that in the process of emphasizing the minutia they were ignoring the important things: righteousness, mercy, and faith.

Since Jesus hit the Pharisees so hard on this issue, you would think that the early church would be fairly free from this problem. But less than 17 years after Christ's ascension, Paul had to go to the church in Jerusalem to straighten out the church leaders. Even those who walked with Jesus were adding to what was required! After much debate, Peter stood up and said, "Now therefore why do you put God to the test by placing upon the neck of the disciples a yoke which neither our fathers nor we have been able to bear?" (Acts 15:10).

Finally the leaders concluded, "For it seemed good to the Holy Spirit and to us to lay upon you no greater burden than these essentials" (Acts 15:28). What was the reaction when the message was sent to all the churches? "And when they had read it, they rejoiced because of its encouragement" (Acts 15:31). The Living Bible says, "And there was great joy throughout the church that day as they read it."

Paul wrote the entire book of Galatians to combat this problem of adding to what is written. He said in Galatians 1:6, "I am amazed that you are so quickly deserting him who called you by the grace of Christ, for a different gospel." Then he put it even more strongly: "But even though we or an angel from heaven should preach to you a gospel contrary to that which we have preached to you, let him be accursed" (Galatians 1:8). He was telling them not to let either respected people or Satan or angels decrease or increase what God has declared in the Bible. Tenaciously hold on to the liberty and grace you have through Jesus Christ!

Modern-Day Examples

Inflicting guilt trips by adding to what is written

occured in both Old Testament and New Testament times. It would be nice to be able to say that the modern-day church is free of such practices, but such is not the case.

Recently a friend related to me his geographical pilgrimage in relation to Christian taboos. When he became a Christian he lived in a community that believed in total abstinence of alcohol, although smoking was an acceptable Christian behavior. And so he conformed.

Then he went to college across the country, and to his amazement smoking was a sin and alcohol was acceptable! So he gave up smoking and learned to enjoy a glass of wine.

Next he was transferred to an area where both of these were serious sins. Wanting to be a good Christian without any guilt, he gave up his glass of wine and grew a beard instead!

This introduces you to some specific things that many churches today convey as laws, but which are not clear-cut in the Bible. I want to be very honest with you and name some of those items. You may not agree with what I'm going to bring up, but I would encourage you to compare what I say to the Scriptures, and not to your past teaching or biases. Paul encourages us to do this in Acts 17:11. If what I say is based on the Scriptures, believe it. If it's not in the Scriptures, don't beleive it. I'm not pointing out these things to haggle over specific issues, but to help you think across the board about the areas within your own Christian life in which subtle, inaccurate teachings may have crept in, teachings that may not be exactly in accordance with the Scriptures.

Let me tell you about Jane. Jane is a 34-year-old divorcee. She's lonely and angry, especially at her ex-husband. Jane came to me for therapy to try to work through some issues, and one that emerged was her very strong sex drive. She said, "It's a problem to me—I don't know how to handle it." So we looked at the options. One option was to get married. She would have been happy to remarry, but Mr. Right wasn't on the horizon, and besides, the divorce was fairly recent. So that option was out for awhile.

We talked about what some might call the "cold shower" approach—grin and bear it. Parenthetically, let me say this about the sexual drive. Some people have very strong sexual drives, others have moderately strong ones, and some couldn't care less. People who are on the "It-doesn't-make-much-difference" end of the spectrum have a very hard time understanding Jane's predicament, and should be careful about judging her. So again, back to the options. The first one, to get married, wasn't an immediate option. The second, to grin and bear it, which she had been doing, hadn't been very satisfactory. She had been questioning whether to have sex, but Jane is a Christian and believes that sex outside of marriage is wrong. She asked if there were any other options.

Well, there was one more option. So we talked about self-stimulation or masturbation. To that consideration she adamantly replied, "Absolutely not!" She didn't even want to talk or think about it. So we dropped the topic and went on to something else. And I've seen this response many times in the past.

But do you know what happened four weeks after that session? Jane had an affair. She even told me, "You know, I don't even like this guy that much, but we're sleeping together."

Jane was in exactly the same dilemma that the Israelites were in when Saul ordered them to fast on the day of battle. The Bible is very clear in stating that sex outside of marriage is contrary to God's will. But the Bible is absolutely silent about masturbation. So Jane, for whatever reason, had a stronger aversion to self-stimulation (on which the Bible is silent) than to sex outside of marriage (on which the Bible is very clear). And a few weeks later she stopped coming to therapy.

This is a common problem, but Christians rarely talk about these things—issues that people struggle with silently, not knowing how to handle them.

The church, because of its silence, tends to imply that masturbation is wrong. The history is long as to where we got this view. Textbooks from the 18th and 19th century graphically describe the horrible things that masturbation would do to you. Blindness, insanity, nervousness, weakness, and hysteria are all ascribed to self-stimulation. And the solutions of that day to masturbation would terrify you if I were to elaborate.

Christian single men in particular agonize over this problem. They want to be committed to God, and they vow, "I won't do it." Then, when the prostate secretions accumulate, there is a biological need for release, so they impulsively masturbate, only to be plagued with guilt. Then their entire Christian life goes down the drain simply because of the guilt over this one issue. You'll seldom hear about it, because the church rarely talks about it. But I hear about it in my office.

There's another area in which we've added to what is written, and I know some of you will have trouble with this. It's the issue of alcohol.

I grew up with the belief that one drop of alcohol used in cooking was sin. There was no in-between category; it was all wrong. I don't believe the Scriptures teach that. There are passages in the Bible indicating that the use of alcohol in moderation is not a sin. In John 2 we read that Jesus' first miracle was turning water into wine, something that He wouldn't have done if He thought drinking wine was wrong. And in 1 Timothy 5:23 Paul tells Timothy, "No longer drink water exclusively, but use a little wine for the sake of your stomach and your frequent ailments."

However, there are also strong injunctions against drinking in excess, such as Ephesians 5:18: "Do not get drunk with wine, for that is dissipation." People who have a problem with alcohol need to stay away from it, and excess is clearly forbidden. But the issue of whether to drink at all is a private matter—between the individual and God.

A third issue is that of restricting certain foods. The Bible says that in latter times men will "advocate abstaining from foods, which God has created to be gratefully shared in by those who believe and know the truth" (1 Timothy 4:3). There is absolutely no Scriptural basis for shunning certain foods for religious reasons.

The Scriptures clearly state what our attitude should be toward such items: "Give a warm welcome to any brother who wants to join you, even though his faith is weak. Don't criticize him for having different ideas from yours about what is right and wrong. For instance, don't argue with him about whether or not to eat meat that has been offered to idols. You may believe there is no harm in this, but the faith of others is weaker; they think it is wrong, and will go without any meat at all and eat vegetables rather than eat that kind of meat. Those who think it is all right to eat such meat must not look down on those who won't. And if you are one of those who won't, don't find fault with those who do. For God has accepted them to be his children. They are God's servants, not yours. They are responsible to him, not to you. Let him tell them whether they are right or wrong." And then this ringing declaration: "On questions of this kind everyone must decide for himself" (Romans 14:1-5 TLB).

With many of these issues, God leaves it up to the individual. He may convict one person to handle it in a certain way and another person in a different way, but we can't make a flat decree for everyone. And we should not impose our personal convictions on someone else.

I should point out that the end of Romans 14 adds a qualifier to our freedom. We are told not to cause someone else to stumble by flaunting our freedom: "It is wrong to eat it if it makes another stumble. The right thing to do is to quit eating meat or drinking wine or doing anything else that offends your brother or makes him sin.... Don't flaunt your faith in front of others who might be hurt by it" (Romans 14:20-22 TLB).

So often, the reason given for not drinking alcohol is that it will cause a brother to stumble. It is my opinion that this rationale has sometimes been used as a club. The big question is *if: if* it causes your brother to stumble. We really need to know whether seeing a Christian with a glass of wine in his hand will actually damage the non-Christian or the sensitive Christian who is watching, and I'm not sure we really know that. "Causing your brother to stumble" is often used to badger other people into conforming to our social standards, whatever they might be.

There's another area in which modern-day Christianity adds to what is written, and that is the tithe. To me, the New Testament is very clear on this issue. Many people would teach or imply that 10 percent of one's income given to God is absolutely required—it's duty. Thus it's sin if one doesn't give God the tithe. What does the common phrase "God's tithe and our offerings" convey? It's subtle, it's low pressure, but it implies that there's a difference between the tithe and the offering. It says that 10 percent should be looked at one way, and 11 or 12 percent should be looked at another way. I don't believe this is consistent with the New Testament.

First Corinthians 16:2 (TLB) says, "On every Lord's Day each of you should put aside something from what you have earned during the week, and use it for this offering. The amount depends on how much the Lord has helped you earn." Or consider 2 Corinthians 9:7 (TLB): "Every one must make up his own mind as to how much he should give. Don't force anyone to give more than he really wants to, for cheerful givers are the ones God prizes."

I believe the Lord is much more pleased with 8 or 9 percent given cheerfully than with 10 or 15 percent given out of duty. God loves cheerful giving, giving out of the abundance of the heart. We're not living under the 613 commands in the Old Testament; we're living under grace. And Paul tells us to hold on to that carefully.

To introduce the next issue, I want to tell you of a patient who we'll call Jackie. Jackie related an incident that occurred when she was 13. Jackie was a sensitive, shy, conscientious new Christian. She was wrestling with her self-esteem. She had thick glasses and was not especially gifted in appearance, personality, or physical coordination. Most of her peers had matured physically; Jackie had not, so she still felt like a little girl. Occasionally she was teased, which was quite a problem for her.

Jackie went to a good church, and had a vivacious, outgoing Sunday school teacher who taught that if you really loved the Lord, you would witness. This only added to Jackie's problems. Sensitive Jackie wrestled with the idea of witnessing to the friends who already were teasing her, and to whom she already felt inferior. She procrastinated, which then heaped more guilt on her sensitive young soul. Before long she became depressed, there was no joy in her Christian life, and eventually she began to question if she was even a Christian. And all this when she was only 13!

Often in recent years, the command has been, "You must witness verbally or you aren't a good Christian." I don't believe that's Scriptural. In the 3½ years that the disciples walked with Jesus, He sent them out on only one missionary trip. The rest of the times we read of no obligation to witness. Finally, at the end of this extensive training period, the disciples were sent out.

Some people are given the gift of evangelism, one of the spiritual gifts. For those who have the gift, God wants them to use it. But not all Christians are given that gift. So we need to be careful how much we stress witnessing, especially to the immature or those who are already dealing with a lot of other problems. You see, there are a lot of Jackies in the world—people who feel they're only 13 even though they may be many times that age and may not seem to have any obvious external problems.

It's true that our lives should be a testimony in and of themselves, as Matthew 5:16 states so clearly: "Let your light shine before men in such a way that they may see your good works and glorify your Father who is in heaven." In addition we are to "Be ready always to give an answer to every man that asketh you a reason of the hope that is in you with meekness and fear" (1 Peter 3:15 KJV). And on an individual basis God may call us to witness verbally.

"We are all called to be missionaries." This was a statement made by a well-known minister. He added, "You are called to the mission field unless you are called not to go." This places an individual in the position of having to prove that God has not called him to the mission field, thus laying on a tremendous burden. This is backward and in error; and I find no Scriptural basis to support it.

6

False Accusations

"Woe to those who call evil good, and good evil, who substitute darkness for light and light for darkness, who substitute bitter for sweet, and sweet for bitter!"

—Isaiah 5:20

*A*nother misuse of guilt is false accusations—trying to get us to believe things which are false. Accusations can come from without, from other people, but often they come from within. Many of the "tapes" that play in our heads are long strings of accusations: "You're so lazy. Look what a fool you made of yourself. You never do anything right. You're always late. You blew it again. How could you be so stupid!"

The Bible says that the Holy Spirit *convicts* us of sin in order to build us up (John 16:8). Satan *accuses* us of false sins in order to tear us down. He is repeatedly referred to in Scripture as "the accuser" or "the adversary," and in the Biblical scenes in which he comes out in the open, he is seen taunting and tormenting people with his accusations.

It is in the book of Job where Satan's accusations are really brought into the limelight. Most of us think of the account of Job as dealing with suffering. Yet I was amazed as I carefully studied the book—*it has more to say about false accusations and guilt trips than suffering.*

We find Satan primarily using the lips of Job's "friends." When they couldn't get Job with one approach, they hit him from another side.

Let's take a brief look at the accusations and Job's responses to them, because he provides us an excellent role model for handling false guilt.

In Job 22 we find one of Job's friends, Eliphaz, saying, "Is it because you are good that he is punishing you? Not at all! It is because of your wickedness! Your sins are endless!... If you give up your lust for money, and throw your gold away," you would be all right (Job 22:4, 5,24 TLB).

Job doesn't buy into this attack. Here is a sampling of his replies: "This is my case: I know that I am righteous" (Job 13:18 TLB). "My righteousness I hold fast, and will not let it go: my heart shall not reproach me so long as I live" (Job 27:6 KJV).

Another accusation that Eliphaz uses in Job 4 and 5 is "Have you ever known a truly good and innocent person who was punished?" (4:7 TLB). "Those who turn from God may be successful for the moment, but then comes sudden disaster" (5:3 TLB). He is using the time-honored guilt trip: If you're suffering adversity, you must have sinned. His advice? "Go to God and confess your sins . . . do not despise the chastening of the Lord when you sin" (5:8,17 TLB). Bildad concurs heartily with him, saying, "The truth remains that if you do not prosper, it is because you are wicked" (18:5 TLB).

Job strongly confronts these false accusations with the terse reply, "Robbers prosper." He adds, "The truth is that the wicked live on to a good old age, and become great and powerful. . . . All this despite the fact that they ordered God away and wanted no part of him and his ways" (12:6; 21:7,14 TLB).

A third approach of the friends is that either God is wrong or Job is. We all know that it couldn't have been God's fault, so who is left? Job, of course. This is an "either-or" argument—no other alternatives are considered. Elihu argues, "Do you really think that if you shout loudly enough against God, he will be ashamed and repent?" (36:19 TLB). In essence he is saying, "Do you think, Job, that God is going to repent if you don't repent?" It is faulty reasoning to state that it had to be *either* God *or* Job who erred.

A modern-day example of this reasoning is the platitude, "If you don't feel close to God, who moved?" The implication is quite obvious—it couldn't be God. But it may be that neither moved. Job said, "Oh, that I knew where to find God!" (23:3 TLB). Job's feeling of being distant from God was a torment to him, and may have been the worst of his trials, but throughout his suffering he maintained his innocence: "I know that after this body has decayed, this body shall see God! Then he will be on *my* side! Yes, I shall see him, not as a stranger, but as a friend! What a glorious hope!" He held on to his eternal hope (19:26,27 TLB).

I'm convinced that God was as interested in Job and as close to him during this trial as before the trial. I'm sure He was looking on in love and compassion, hurting when Job hurt. Simply *feeling* that God is far away doesn't alter the facts—it doesn't necessarily mean that anyone has moved. Our feelings may go up and down, but *they are not necessarily indicative of our relationship with God.*

The next approach that Job's accusers use is "You could have done more," reminiscent of the "more is better" philosophy discussed earlier in this book. Eliphaz said, "You must have refused to loan money to needy friends. . . . You must have refused water to the thirsty, and bread to the starving. . . . You sent widows away without helping them" (22:6-9 TLB).

Again, Job maintains his innocence. He says that God "knows every detail of what is happening to me; and when he has examined me, he will pronounce me completely innocent—as pure as solid gold! I have stayed in God's paths, following his steps. I have not turned aside . . . his mind concerning me remains unchanged" (23:10-13 TLB).

Elihu makes one last-ditch effort: "Do not desire the nighttime, with its opportunities for crime. Turn back from evil, for it was to prevent you from getting into a life of evil that God sent this suffering" (36:20,21 TLB). In other words, if you haven't done anything wrong up to now, Job, God is giving you this suffering to prevent you from sin in the future.

At this point God finally intervenes and says to Eliphaz, "I am angry with you and your two friends, for you have not been right in what you said about me, as my servant Job was" (42:7 TLB). So God Himself affirms Job's innocence. Then God has Job pray for his friends who had been his accusers, and "he restored his wealth and happiness!" (42:10 TLB).

There's another thing to note about those who make false accusations: They often get angry and accuse us of what they themselves are doing. Elihu "became angry because Job refused to admit he had sinned and to acknowledge that God had just cause for punishing him" (32:2 TLB). And in Job 20:3 (TLB) Zophar became defensive, saying, "You have tried to make me feel ashamed of myself for calling you a sinner, but my spirit won't let me stop."

Another thing to notice is how chronic and unrelenting the attacks were. We are not told how long a period of time this testing took. Possibly it was many weeks or months. I have wondered if the most difficult task Job had to face was not losing his family, possessions, or health, but having to stand firm against the constant barrage of accusations and false guilt. In chapter 19:2 (TLB) Job cries out, "How long are you going to trouble me, and try to break me with your words?''

It's the same today. The old saying ''Sticks and stones may break my bones, but words can never hurt me'' just isn't true. I'm convinced more and more as I see people in my office that words can indeed hurt—it is the *words* that break the spirit of so many people.

It is my hope that we can see the mechanism people use to lay false guilt on us, and can learn from the way Job handled them. Job refused to let his friends accuse him and lay guilt trips on him, and that's precisely what we need to do with false accusations today, both from without and within.

Job stood firm in his faith in God and his belief in his innocence, and he didn't allow the loss of health, adverse circumstances, or false accusations to shake his stand.

MODERN-DAY FALSE ACCUSATIONS

The issue of put-downs or judging is an important one. Christians tend to use put-downs which say, ''I'm more spiritual than you are.'' No one ever says it in those words, but that's what is implied. A person may tell of some ecstatic spiritual experience he has had, implying that you ought to have a similar supernatural experience.

Recently I heard someone say, ''He's not filled with the Holy Spirit.'' Or there's the one, ''You aren't really Spirit-filled unless you speak in tongues.'' If you read through the Scriptures you will find that every conversion was different, and not everybody had ecstatic experiences. In regard to spiritual gifts, the Bible says: "But one and the same Spirit works all these things, distributing to each one individually just as He wills" (1 Corinthians 12:11). So people with one particular gift shouldn't judge those who haven't been given that gift.

I've seen people hurt because someone has told them that they haven't been healed because they don't have enough faith. Paul Tournier speaks about this issue in his book *Guilt and Grace:*

> I cannot study this very serious problem of guilt with you without raising the very obvious and tragic fact that religion—my own as well as that of all believers—can crush instead of liberate. There is a kind of unavoidable reverse side to every declaration of faith, which follows it as faithfully as shadow follows sunshine. To say that one has found truth in Roman Catholic doctrine or in Reformed doctrine, in Pentecostalism or in Adventism implies to those who do not share our faith that we consider them as lost in error (p. 23).

Again we have to come back to Romans 14, which emphasizes, "Don't let anyone else judge you." One of the most harmful things that we as Christians do to our brothers and sisters in Christ is to pass judgment on them, even if we do it with seemingly harmless innuendos.

Some people think they've committed the un-

pardonable sin, that of blaspheming the Holy
Spirit (Matthew 12:31,32). However, everyone
I've talked to who worries about this has been
a sensitive person desiring to do God's will,
hardly a likely candidate for blasphemy. They
are either hypersensitive people or are being ac-
cused by Satan (Revelation 12:10).

However, I also think that we in the church
have viewed certain sins as being worse than
others—as being virtually unpardonable. Oh, we
would never say it, but we act it out by never
really pardoning certain people. Divorcees are
often placed in this category.

I can see a new unpardonable sin lurking
on the horizon—abortion. I am reminded of a
patient of mine who attends a well-known
church in Southern California. She was in
turmoil because she thought she was pregnant—and she was single. After she discovered
she wasn't, she told me, "You know, I have
fought for the prolife, antiabortion issue, but
if I had been pregnant I would have had an
abortion because where I go to church, I would
have been a marked person for the rest of
my life." How sad. I believe we as Christians
must be very careful not to regard other Christians as being permanently tainted because
of something in their past which God has
forgiven.

We Christians need to be as forgiving as God
is, and this is precisely where our problem lies.
We often aren't as forgiving to ourselves and to
one another as God is to us.

THE GUILT OF CHRISTIANS

God desires a guilt-free life for us, but it is so easy, especially for Christians, to accumulate large amounts of guilt. Let me try to clarify why it is that Christians often suffer with more guilt than non-Christians.

If we were to diagram the non-Christian's guilt system, this is how it would look:

Non-Christian

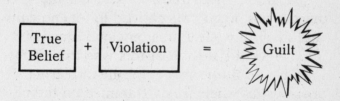

True Belief + Violation = Guilt

God has made all people aware of His universal laws. It is also a fact that all people have violated these universal laws. The Bible says, "All have sinned and fall short of the glory of God" (Romans 3:23). The guilt they have is then valid guilt, based on God's valid laws. So the non-Christian has some unresolved guilt. But since everyone can tolerate a certain amount of guilt and still get by, most people carry on fairly well.

When a person becomes a Christian, the

diagram changes to this:

New Christian

$$\boxed{\begin{array}{c}\text{True}\\\text{Belief}\end{array}} \quad + \quad 0 \quad = \quad \begin{array}{c}\text{No}\\\text{Guilt}\end{array}$$

(All violations of
beliefs forgiven)

The valid beliefs are still there, but because this person has accepted Christ's payment for his violations, he is free from sin's penalty. This person has no guilt, is entitled to feel no guilt, and hopefully is walking on cloud nine. And I remember the night that this was true of me.

However, as the years pass, the Christian adds more valid beliefs, as diagrammed on the next page with a larger box. This is because the person has been a Christian for awhile, and knows more of what God expects of him, and is held responsible for that knowledge.

But all too often what happens is that conscientious Christians begin accumulating false beliefs, all the do's and don't's of their particular Christian cultures. This person inevitably violates some of them and also some of the true beliefs, because he usually doesn't know how to differentiate between them. The inevitable result is that the guilt increases, as diagrammed on the next page.

Older Christians

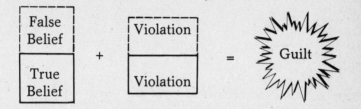

God's ideal for us—such a simple way of life in comparison—is diagrammed below:

God's Ideal:

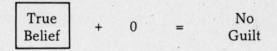

(All violations of
beliefs forgiven)

The box of true beliefs may indeed be much larger, but God has promised to give us the resources to keep His commandments (1 Corinthians 10:13, 1 John 5:3). And if we do violate God's standards, provisions have been made for that, which will be covered in the next chapter.

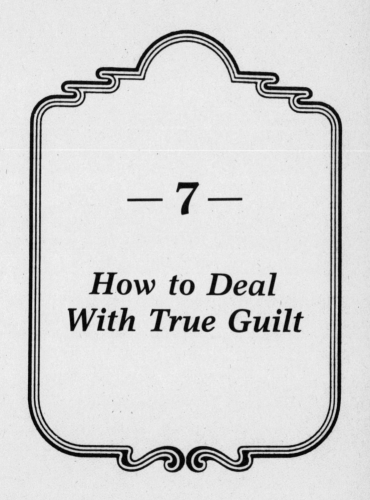

— 7 —

How to Deal
With True Guilt

OUR BASIC ALIENATION

*F*or some who may be reading this book, the first step in dealing with guilt may not be an easy one to face. You must come to grips with your basic alienation from God.

The Bible states that all of us are basically self-centered individuals, living life for ourselves and ignoring God. In the Old Testament we are depicted as sheep who have wandered away from the Shepherd: "All of us like sheep have gone astray; each of us has turned to his own way" (Isaiah 53:6a). It is this self-centeredness that keeps us at odds with God and His plan for our lives.

Side-stepping this issue or refusing to acknowledge that it exists at all can keep us from ever understanding God's will for us. By our self-centeredness we are basically thumbing our noses at God: "I'm okay, God—I'm doing fine without You." But we are *not* doing fine without Him. We are sinful without Him; we are truly guilty. And if we do not accept His diagnosis of our basic human nature, we will be unable to apply His remedy.

To continue with the passage quoted on the previous page: "But the Lord has caused the iniquity of us all to fall on Him [Christ]" (Isaiah 53:6b). So the only way to be guilt-free is to believe that Christ died for our sins. If He had not done this, we would all stand guilty before God. But in His grace, God accepts Christ's death as payment for our sin and removes our guilt. This is where we must begin in order to live a guilt-free life.

If you are not sure whether you have accepted Christ's provision for your sin, please consider the following principles.

The Bible clearly teaches that God loves and cares for each one of us. Jeremiah 31:3 says that He has "loved you with an everlasting love" and is drawing us to Himself with "lovingkindness." The Bible also teaches that God has a plan for our lives and desires that we each experience a fulfilled life with personal peace—a peace and fulfillment that only He can give. This is why Christ came to earth some 2000 years ago to live, die, and be raised from the dead—so that we "might have life, and might have it abundantly" (John 10:10).

When man first sinned in the Garden of Eden, God pronounced the death sentence on all mankind. And since all have sinned all suffer its consequences (see Romans 5:12). In other words, we all deserve eternal death. Since only an innocent person can take on the penalty of a guilty person, Christ, the sinless One, took our sentence for us, dying in our place. But after three days God raised Him from the dead, conquering sin and death. "For Christ also died for sins once for all, the just for the unjust, in order that He might bring us to God" (1 Peter 3:18).

But we must appropriate God's gift by personally accepting what Christ has done for us. One of the most familiar verses in the Bible puts it this way: "For God so loved the world that he gave his only begotten Son, that whosoever believeth in him should not perish but have everlasting life" (John 3:16 KJV). Thus accepting Christ involves a definite choice on our part.

If you have not experienced the assurance of peace with God that comes through accepting His diagnosis and remedy for your sin and your guilt, I would encourage you to say a simple prayer, expressing faith in God and thanking Him for what He has done for you through Christ.

TRUE GUILT

Ideally, once we have dealt with our basic alienation from God by accepting Christ, we shouldn't need to sin again, and therefore this section shouldn't be necessary. However, in actuality we all "blow it," make mistakes, or sin in some way. Regardless of what we call it, we violate God's laws and therefore experience the pain of guilt (Romans 7:14-25; 1 John 2:1). This is the guilt that we face as Christians, and subsequently I will refer to this as *true guilt*. We need to know how to handle this guilt when we sin.

When we feel guilty, the first thing we need to do is to ask ourselves, "What am I feeling guilty about?" Then, as best we can, we must try to pinpoint it. We may need to pray and ask the Lord for insight, we may need to take a piece of paper and write down all the possibilities, or we may need to talk it over with a friend. We must also be willing to face whatever facts are revealed to us, even if they are unpleasant.

The next step is to examine whether the underlying belief that is fueling the guilt is valid or not—whether it is *true guilt* or *false guilt*. These are the first steps: Determine that 1) "I'm feeling guilty!" 2) "What is it about?" 3) "Is it valid guilt or not?"

If we decide that it is valid guilt, we need to remember that *true belief plus a violation leads to true guilt.* God wants to free us of this true guilt, and we find the remedy He has provided for us in 1 John 1:9: "If we confess our sins, He is faithful and righteous to forgive us our sins and to cleanse us from all unrighteousness."

What exactly does it mean to "confess"? Confession simply means to agree with God that we have disobeyed Him, and that we are truly sorry for it—we can't be indifferent or flippant. It means that our intention is to change in that area. Notice that I say *intention* I'm not saying that we're promising never to slip up in that area again, because it's possible that we might. Jesus told us to forgive other people "seventy times seven," and God has certainly forgiven us at least 490 times! What He wants is that we express true sorrow for that sin, and become willing to let Him help us change in that area. Note also that it is *God* who helps us change. The whole message of the Bible is "Apart from Me you can do nothing" (John 15:5).

Psalm 32:3-5 describes the process of confession: "When I kept silent about my sin, my body wasted away through my groaning all day long. For day and night Thy hand was heavy upon me; my vitality was drained away as with the fever heat of summer. I acknowledged my sin to Thee, and my iniquity I did not hide; I said, 'I will confess my transgressions to the Lord'; and Thou didst forgive the guilt of my sin."

Psalm 51 is another beautiful passage describing the process of confession and forgiveness:

> Be gracious to me, O God, according to
>   Thy lovingkindness;
> According to the greatness of Thy com-
>   passion blot out my trangressions.
> Wash me thoroughly from my iniquity,
> And cleanse me from my sin.
>
> For I know my transgressions,
> And my sin is ever before me.
> Against Thee, Thee only, I have sinned....
> Behold, Thou dost desire truth in the
>   innermost being....
>
> Purify me...and I shall be clean;
> Wash me, and I shall be whiter than snow.
> Make me to hear joy and gladness....

> Hide Thy face from my sins,
>
> And blot out all my iniquities.
> Create in me a clean heart, O God,
> And renew a steadfast spirit within
> me....
> Restore to me the joy of Thy salvation.
> —Psalm 51:1-4,6,7,9,10,12

How does God view us after we have admitted our sins? Jesus said to the repentant adulteress in John 8:11, "Neither do I condemn you; go your way. From now on sin no more." This is God's message when we come to Him and confess our sin. Hebrews 10:17 says, "Their sins and their lawless deeds I will remember no more."

The steps in dealing with true guilt are diagrammed on the opposite page.

"Is that all?" you might ask. "It almost seems too easy. Don't I need to do anything else?"

Basically the answer is no. God has forgiven you, and that is that. All that is left is to claim and cling to that fact, not allowing Satan to tempt you into doubting God's forgiveness.

Some people still think that this is too easy. Don't we need to make up for our wrongdoing somehow—don't we need to ask those we've wronged to forgive us? Don't we need to rectify any damage done by our actions?

There are some well-known Christian leaders who teach that we need to do more, that we need to make confession to other people and offer restitution. One leader says that in order to

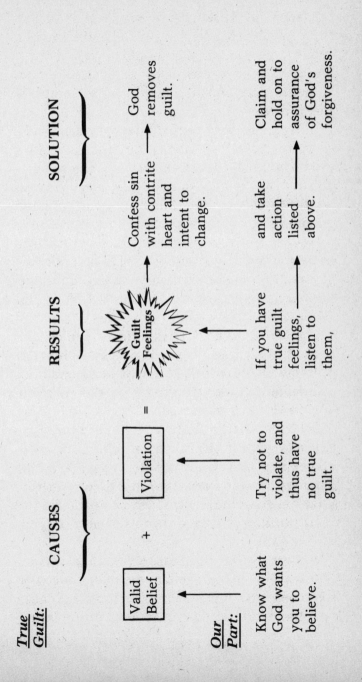

True Guilt:

CAUSES

Valid Belief + Violation = **RESULTS**

Guilt Feelings → **SOLUTION**

Confess sin with contrite heart and intent to change. → God removes guilt.

Our Part:

Know what God wants you to believe. → Try not to violate, and thus have no true guilt. → If you have true guilt feelings, listen to them, → and take action listed above. → Claim and hold on to assurance of God's forgiveness.

have a clear conscience, we should go back to the person we have wronged and make amends. If we have stolen, we should own up to the truth; if we've lost our tempers or said something unkind, we should try to somehow make it right.

In trying to answer this question, the crucial thing to realize is that sin is primarily against God. David said in Psalm 51:4, "Against Thee, Thee only, I have sinned" (see also Genesis 39:9). When we confess our sin, God forgives! He doesn't demand that we make restitution as a condition for forgiveness. I believe we need to be aware of the subtle feeling that confession and restitution are necessary for God's forgiveness—this borders on trying to atone for our sins, when Christ has already done this.

I believe that the only situation in which confession to another person is necessary is when you have truly wronged that person, and your wrongdoing is keeping him from a right relationship with God or yourself. This is when Matthew 5:23,24 is applicable: "If therefore you are presenting your offering at the altar, and there remember that your brother has something against you, leave your offering there before the altar, and go your way; first be reconciled to your brother, and then come and present your offering."

Sometimes the real reason we make amends is that we need to flagellate ourselves; we need to do penance or we need to get it off our chest. Sometimes our purpose in "confessing" to some-

one else is really to dump our load of guilt on
him. A 52-year-old patient of mine was in a great
deal of turmoil about a number of things, one
of which was an affair that happened 28 years
earlier, in the first year of her marriage. In her
desire to get rid of this guilt, she poured it all
out on her poor husband, which created tremendous havoc in their relationship. This action did
neither of them any good.

What about restitution? The Old Testament
teaches: "Thus you shall not show pity: life for
life, eye for eye, tooth for tooth, hand for hand,
foot for foot" (Deuteronomy 19:21). It also tells
us that when we cheat someone, we should offer a guilt offering to God and make full restitution to the person we've cheated, plus 20 percent more (Leviticus 5:7; 6:5).

But what does the New Testament teach? Is
there ever a command to pay restitution? In the
account of Zacchaeus, the tax collector, Luke
19:6-8 says that he volunteered to make restitution, but he wasn't ordered to by Jesus. Out of
joy he said, "Behold, Lord, half of my possessions I will give to the poor, and if I have
defrauded anyone of anything, I will give back
four times as much." Jesus didn't encourage or
discourage Zacchaeus; He just said, "Today
salvation has come to this house." He saw the
man's heart.

The disciple Matthew also was a tax collector.
Tax collectors were notorious for defrauding
people, for collecting more than was due and
keeping the rest for themselves. But when Jesus

called Matthew to be His disciple, He didn't say,
"Pay restitution and follow me. He simply said,
"Follow me" (Mark 2:14).

Ephesians 4:28 says, "Let him who steals steal
no longer, but rather let him labor." It doesn't
say, let him make restitution for all he has stolen.
It says, let him *steal no longer*—a change, a
turning around.

The Holy Spirit might, on an individual basis,
lead a person to restore a stolen item. For example, if you have a stolen tennis racket in your
closet and you know whom it belongs to and can
easily return it, it's very possible that God may
lay it on your heart to return it.

However, let me share my experience in this
regard. This incident took place when I was 19,
during that period of time which I've already
described in previous chapters. As I became
more and more exhausted, some sins from years
past came back to haunt me—stealing something
from a drugstore, lying to my father, and a
third thing which I can't even remember today.
As I would pray, these three things would prey
on my mind, and I would wonder if I should
confess to these people. Then I had to wrestle
with my unwillingness to face up to these
people.

Finally I said, in my exhaustion, "Lord, I'll do
anything—I'll confess, I'll pay restitution, I'll do
whatever You want." I decided to go to a Christian leader for advice, and he told me to confess and ask forgiveness of the three people.

So with lump in throat I marched out to do

my duty. At the time I felt I was doing the right thing, but now as I look back, I think that in my weariness Satan had dredged up some old things and created this turmoil in my hypersensitive conscience. I knew of no way to get rid of the turmoil except to go to the three people and confess.

But in retrospect, I'm not sure I needed to do that. I think what I needed was for someone to remind me that God had already forgiven me. I think that Satan, the "accuser of the brethren," was having a field day with me, keeping me in a state of tremendous internal conflict (Revelation 12:10).

We flagellate ourselves because we can't forgive ourselves. *The Comprehensive Textbook of Psychiatry* says, "When a person 'feels guilty' . . . he ordinarily attempts to make restitution." You can look at what tribes in the remote parts of the earth do to assuage their guilt—they sacrifice their children, they torture themselves. Or look at Adam and Eve when they tried to cover their shame with fig leaves, thinking that maybe in some way it would put them right with God.

Man has always attempted to make restitution for his own sin. It is a deep-seated tendency that may not necessarily go away when a person becomes a Christian. Often the attempts of restitution are really our offerings for our sins. We are trying to make it up to God when we simply don't need to.

Let's look at it realistically. If we tried to make

amends to every person for the hurts we inflicted on him or her, there is no way we could do it. We would spend untold hours dredging up past sins and trying to rectify them. We would be obsessed with the negative and prone to worry that we might have missed something. Furthermore, we would become hypersensitive to new infractions. In it all our focus would be on sin instead of the Savior.

So I see restitution, and often confession, as basically a voluntary matter. At times the law might make us pay restitution; sometimes the person injured might. But I don't believe it is a New Testament principle. The essence of New Testament theology is that Christ was our once-and-for-all offering for sin. Hebrews 10:18 declares, "Now where there is forgiveness of these things, there is no longer any offering for sin."

8

How to Deal With False Guilt

*I*t was two o'clock on a Friday afternoon. I was running some errands, and when I drove by Gemco, a local department store, I decided to go in. There wasn't any shopping I *had* to do—I was just browsing.

All of a sudden I felt very anxious, as though something was wrong, and noticed that I was even perspiring a little. Then I realized that underneath those uncomfortable feelings was a vague sense of guilt. But why?

At this point in the procedure of dealing with guilt, all we can conclude is that I felt guilty and had the urge to leave the store. My body was reacting to some belief that was being violated. The feelings were exactly the same at that moment regardless of whether it was a true or false belief that was being violated.

The feeling that arises from both true and false guilt are absolutely identical. That's why in differentiating between true and false guilt, you can't go by the feelings. Feelings are just the flashing yellow light. They are the warning to be careful, to take inventory—that's all they say.

Once I have determined that I am feeling guilty, I must pinpoint exactly what it's about. If I had scheduled a 2 P.M. appointment, it would have been true guilt, and I should heed the feeling and take corrective action, (i.e., drive quickly to my office). However, the feelings of guilt were really old "tapes" saying, "You should be working. You shouldn't be wasting time browsing even though you have Friday afternoons off."

False guilt feelings crop up when we violate a belief that we consciously or unconsciously believe to be true, when in reality it's not one of God's commands, but rather one that man has made. It may be a command or an injunction from a parent that is not valid for us, or an injunction that any other authority has established and which we've accepted as true, perhaps without our even being aware of its existence.

First John 4:1 TLB says, "Dearly loved friends, don't always believe everything you hear just because someone says it is a message from God; test it first to see if it really is." Colossians 2:16 puts it quite bluntly: "Therefore let no one act as your judge." Paul himself encouraged even his own listeners to compare what he was teaching with the Scriptures, to see if what he preached was true (see Acts 17:11).

When Satan tempted Jesus in Matthew 4, three times Jesus rebutted his argument with Scripture. But in the last temptation Satan went so far as to quote Scripture out of context. Christ countered him with the appropriate use of Scripture. Thus even the Bible can be twisted to support a lie, an accusation, or a false belief.

Once we have determined that the guilt

feelings are due to false guilt, how do we deal with the feelings? The most important thing to realize is that our emotions have a hard time catching up with our intellect. Knowing that feelings are the result of false guilt doesn't ensure that those uncomfortable feelings will immediately vanish. So what do we do in the meantime?

Basically, there are three options: The first is to become callous to guilt. But if we become numb to false guilt, we will also become numb to true guilt feelings and eventually all feelings, such as happiness and joy. So that is obviously not a healthy option.

The second option is to avoid violating the false belief—to use our earlier example, to never browse in Gemco or in any other way "waste" time on Friday afternoons. This is the way many people handle false guilt feelings year after year, without even realizing it. They always try to stay one step ahead of it. However, this is actually the easy way out. It's avoiding the issue rather than dealing with it. And in fact it becomes a way to feed guilt, by letting it bend you into perpetual submission.

The third and most difficult option is to deal with the false guilt feelings head-on. This is the most constructive option, and gets you out of the situation of being blindly led by your feelings.

My prototype for dealing with false guilt feelings is the same as that for dealing with a phobic anxiety. Let me illustrate with Joan, who is terrified of elevators. When she was three years old she was put in a large box by her brother, who then sat on it. At seven years of age she was locked in a trunk by the same brother. At 15 she rode in a squeaky elevator that jerked a little. She became terrified, thinking she was trapped in it, and progressively she developed more anxiety about riding elevators, so avoided them whenever possible. Years later she came to see me, unable even to step into an elevator. How do you deal with this?

Well, you try to help her understand where the fear originated—to help her see that it's irrational, that it's a false belief. But Joan is still terrified of elevators. She knows in her head that it's irrational to be so afraid, but the fear is so intense that she feels as though she's going to die even if she thinks about one. So what you need to do is to desensitize her.

The first step in desensitizing her is to say, "Now, Joan, I just want you to think about an elevator."

"Oh, no—I don't even want to think about it," she says, terrorized at the mere suggestion.

"What did the last elevator you saw look like?" I ask. "What color was the door? Where was the button?"

Well, she manages to decribe it, but is obviously very uncomfortable. Then I send her home the first week with the assignment of spending five minutes every day thinking about an elevator. It sounds ridiculous, but that's what I do. Gradually her anxiety decreases, so I move on to the next step. If there is an elevator in the building I say, "Let's go over to the elevator—let's just look at it."

"Oh, no—I don't need to look at an elevator," she protests. But eventually she is able to look at the elevator, and then her assignment is to visit an elevator every day, just to look at it.

The third step of desensitization is to go to an elevator once a day and push the button. The following step is to push the button and let the door open without getting in; then to walk in and out without closing the door. And so the process continues. Gradually the patient is desensitized of the phobic fear that elevators are like coffins which they could get trapped in and die.

The same process can be used to desensitize a person of false guilt feelings. You have to work at counteracting what you have been falsely taught.

There is an example of desensitization in the Scriptures. The Jews were commanded in the law not to eat certain animals because they were considered "unclean." When God abolished the law, He made salvation available to the Gentile, although the Jews didn't realize it yet (see Romans chapters 9-11).

Acts 10 relates that a group of Gentiles were gathered at the home of Cornelius, and God wanted Peter to share the gospel with them. This was something previously unheard of, since Jews didn't mingle with Gentiles. So God had to get the message through to Peter that the Gentiles were not "unclean," and God's way of doing that was to show Peter that "unclean" animals were now "clean."

In a dreamlike state Peter saw a sheet come down from heaven with "all kinds of four-footed animals and crawling creatures and birds of the air." Three times a voice said, "Arise, Peter, kill and eat!" And three times Peter said, "By no means, Lord, for I have never eaten anything unholy and unclean."

The voice then replied, "What God has cleansed, no longer consider unholy."

Immediately after this there was a knock on the door—a messenger came asking for Peter to visit Cornelius. Finally Peter understood the meaning of his vision: He was being desensitized of guilt from his old belief that Gentiles were unclean. And through this avenue the gospel was brought to the Gentiles.

So how do I desensitize myself from feeling guilty about "wasting" time in Gemco? Having decided it was false guilt, I "desensitized" myself by browsing a little longer. And after awhile my uncomfortable feelings decreased and I left.

False guilt often leads you into impossible situations. This is another reason why it's so important to be fully aware of false guilt, and thus not to cater to it. The new bride who was taught that she must please everyone soon finds herself in impossible situations. If her mother wants her to go to the church potluck Tuesday night, but her husband wants her to go to the game with him, she will feel guilty for not pleasing one of them, regardless of her decision.

Or there is the person who feels he must be perfect. The message from his parents was, "If you're good enough, I'll love you." So he tries harder and harder to be that perfect child. But because none of us is perfect, the situation becomes impossible. What needs to be done is to deal with the false belief that he must be perfect in order to be loved by his parents, by other people, by God, and most of all by himself.

The diagram below summarizes how to deal with false guilt:

False Guilt:

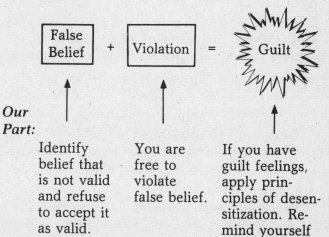

Our Part:

Identify belief that is not valid and refuse to accept it as valid.

You are free to violate false belief.

If you have guilt feelings, apply principles of desensitization. Remind yourself that you haven't committed any sin, and that you remain in God's grace.

In summary, false guilt arises when a false belief is violated. Once we have determined that a belief is false, we are free to violate it (1 Peter 2:16). This doesn't mean that we *must* violate the false belief, but that we have that option. If we want to break the effect of false guilt *feelings*, we must understand the origin of the false belief and undergo desensitization.

SUMMARY ON RESOLVING GUILT

The first thing to do if you have guilt feelings is to ask yourself what it is that is making you feel guilty. If it is more than one thing, try to pinpoint each and every one.

The next questions is, "Is it true or false guilt? Has a true or false belief been violated?"

Let's assume that it's a valid belief, that you're violating some valid command. Then you must admit to God that you've sinned, with a contrite heart and with the intent to change your ways.

You then need to accept the fact that you're forgiven. God promises to forgive, and it's up to you to claim and to cling to that promise of His forgiveness.

That's the way to resolve *true* guilt.

The first step in resolving *false* guilt is to refuse to accept the false belief. The next step is to refuse to yield to the feelings, and the last step is to desensitize yourself of them.

How should we handle our guilt if we don't know whether it is true or false? Certainly it would be wise to pray and ask the Lord to reveal what is happening, to help sort out the facts, and to direct our thinking. Then we should determine what parts don't fit into the true or the false category. Sometimes we're in a muddled situation in which some parts are clearly true guilt and other parts are clearly false guilt. There also may be some other parts that we just can't figure out. The place to start is on what we clearly know to be true or false guilt.

If we've done all this, and everything still seems foggy, what then? Romans 14 tells us that when we are unsure about an issue, we have to act as if it were a valid belief for the time being. "I know and am convinced in the Lord Jesus that nothing is unclean in itself," Paul says in verse 14, talking about meat that had been sacrificed to idols. He has already stated that it is no sin to eat that meat; it is just how a person views it.

But then he adds, "But to him who thinks anything to be unclean, to him it is unclean" (verse 14). Notice that he said *thinks,* not *feels.* Further along in the passage he says, "But he who doubts is condemned if he eats, because his eating is not from faith; and whatever is not from faith is sin" (verse 23).

The New English Bible renders this verse, "But a man who has doubts is guilty if he eats, because his action does not arise from his conviction, and anything which does not arise from conviction is sin."

A good example is the much-debated issue of alcohol. Even though Paul told Timothy to drink a little wine for his health (1 Timothy 5:23), many people still believe that all use of alcohol is wrong. If you *believe* that it is wrong, then

Summary of How to Resolve Guilt

Steps:

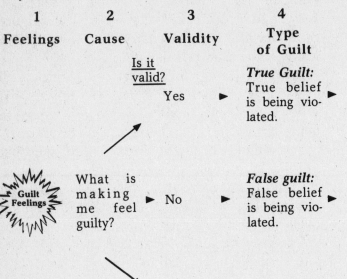

1	2	3	4
Feelings	Cause	Validity	Type of Guilt

<u>Is it valid?</u>

Yes

True Guilt: True belief is being violated. ►

What is making me feel guilty? ► No

False guilt: False belief is being violated. ►

Not sure

Unknown: Don't know whether it's true or false belief being violated. ►

5	6	7
Action	**Result**	**Goal**
• Admit you have sinned to God, with contrite heart and intent to change. ▶	God promises forgiveness —claim and cling to that fact.	
• Do not accept false belief as true one. ▶ • Don't yield to guilt feelings. • Desensitize guilt feelings. • Erase old tapes.		Freedom from guilt through God's grace: "Blessed, happy, to be envied is he who has no reason to judge himself for what he approves— who does not convict himself by what he chooses to do" (Romans 14:22, AMP).
• Deal with components that are clearly true or false guilt. ▶ • Pray. • Study the Bible. • Get counsel. • If still unsure, go along with the belief for the time being as if it were valid.		

you have to *act* as if that is a valid belief, and not touch alcohol. It doesn't mean that all use of alcohol is a sin in the sight of God, but *for you personally* it is a sin. You then have to live that way until such a time as your belief changes on the issue, realizing that it may never change. Just one word of caution: Be careful not to make a general rule for everyone from your own personal conviction.

Going through these steps to rid ourselves of guilt leads to God's grace, forgiveness, and blessing. The Amplified Version of Romans 14:22 says, "Blessed, happy, to be envied is he who has no reason to judge himself for what he approves—who does not convict himself by what he chooses to do." The way we are happy and blessed and able to live in God's grace is if our actions coincide with our beliefs, and if our beliefs are based on the Scriptures. And God tells us in 1 John 5:3 that the commands in the Scriptures are not burdensome.

9

Preventing Unnecessary Guilt

GOD'S WORD AS THE STANDARD

Knowing God's Word is crucial in dealing with guilt, because the Bible alone gives us a standard for our true beliefs. The reason that secular psychologists have so much difficulty dealing with guilt is that they have no absolute standard. Because of that, they tend to call all guilt "neurotic" guilt, and simply try to somehow do away with it.

The only time secular psychology acknowledges the need for guilt is in the case of a person with a character disorder, such as a hardened criminal. Then they say this person doesn't have enough guilt. Other than that, they tend to ignore the hard fact that there is true and false guilt, because they have no ultimate standard. For me, the standard is the Word of God. And if this is the standard by which I judge things, then I've got to really know the Scriptures.

There are many Biblical examples that show the importance of knowing God's Word. When David recaptured the ark of God from the

Philistines, he carried it back to Jerusalem on a cart pulled by oxen (2 Samuel 6). The ark started to fall off the cart, and a man named Uzzah tried to rescue it by grabbing it and steadying it. He was immediately struck dead by God.

David became confused and angry about this, because it seemed that Uzzah was doing the right thing, and here he was killed for it. When I first read that account, I also was confused—why did God do this? After all, the man's motives were right.

It took awhile for me to discover where the problem lay: The ark was not being transported the way God had commanded. It was to be carried by poles inserted through rings in the corners of the ark. And the whole purpose of carrying it this way was to ensure that no one would ever touch it, or else they would die. Uzzah was struck because he touched a holy object, which violated one of God's most fundamental laws (see Numbers 4:15; Exodus 25:14; 1 Chronicles 15:15).

This situation wouldn't have come up in the first place if David had studied the law, as he was commanded. The kings were commanded, "Now it shall come about when he [the king] sits on the throne of his kingdom, he shall write for himself a copy of this law on a scroll in the presence of the Levitical priests. And it shall be with him, and he shall read it all the days of his life, that he may learn to fear the Lord his God, by carefully observing all the words of this law

and these statutes. . . that he may not turn aside
from the commandment, to the right or the left''
(Deuteronomy 17:18-20).

Notice that it wasn't the priests who were
to write the laws, but *the king* who was to write
them out in longhand. Hundreds of years before
Israel even had kings, the kings of the future
were commanded to have their own personal
scroll of the Word of God that they themselves
had written out, and they were to read it every
day.

If David had done that, he would have known
how the ark was to be carried. In the same way,
we so often get into trouble because we don't
know what the Scriptures really say about a
given issue.

In the middle of Colossians where it warns us
not to make unnecessary rules about eating meat
and observing holidays, it also urges us to have
full knowledge of the mysteries of God in Christ,
to be ''firmly rooted'' and ''built up in Him''
(Colossians 2:6,7). We do this through knowing
the Word of God.

Or consider 1 Timothy 4. Paul warns his
readers about false teachers—men who have an
insensitive, seared conscience. This is followed
with preventive advice: to be ''constantly
nourished on the words of the faith and of the
sound doctrine,'' and to ''give attention to the
public reading of Scripture, to exhortation and
teaching'' (1 Timothy 4:6,13). Again, we need
to be rooted firmly in Scripture.

In John 8:31,32 Jesus says, ''If you abide in

My word, then you are truly disciples of Mine; and you shall know the truth, and the truth shall make you free." Thus, knowing and following the Scriptures are necessary ingredients to being a follower of Christ. This also is the means for knowing the truth, "and the truth shall make you free"—free from guilt, too.

The Book of Hebrews points out the relationship between knowing the deeper aspects of God's Word (referred to in this passage as "solid food") and discerning right from wrong: "For everyone who partakes only of milk is not accustomed to the word of righteousness, for he is a babe. But solid food is for the mature, who because of practice have their senses trained to discern good and evil" (Hebrews 5:13,14).

If we're going to have a handle on guilt, we've got to have a handle on the Word of God; otherwise, we have no standard for judging right from wrong.

PRAYER AND THE HOLY SPIRIT

"But if any of you lacks wisdom, let him ask of God, who gives to all men generously" (James 1:5). Both in studying Scripture and in applying it to our lives, we need to ask God for the wisdom and strength to do His will. Proverbs 3:6 commands, "In all thy ways acknowledge him, and he shall direct thy paths" (KJV).

God uses the Holy Spirit in our lives as counselor, teacher, and guide (see John 14:16,26;

16:13). It is the Holy Spirit who instructs us as to what is right. Paul says in Romans 9:1, "I am speaking the truth as a Christian, and my own conscience, enlightened by the Holy Spirit, assures me" (NEB).

KEEPING THINGS IN PERSPECTIVE

The first thing to emphasize when trying to keep things in perspective is to love God. When Jesus was asked what the most important commandment was, He replied, " 'Love the Lord your God with all your heart, soul, and mind.' This is the first and greatest commandment. The second most important is similar: 'Love your neighbor as much as you love yourself . . . . Keep only these and you will find that you are obeying all the others' " (Matthew 22:37-40 TLB).

Let me emphasize that last statement: Keep only these and you will find that you are obeying all the others. Christ is saying that if you emphasize loving God first, and then loving other people as much as you love yourself, you will have all the commandments in their proper perspective. And I maintain that if this commandment isn't kept in perspective—if we start emphasizing any other command, no matter how good—we begin distorting God's commands. There is such a strong tendency to get our priorities mixed up by emphasizing secondary issues, and in the process lose sight of the primary things that God is emphasizing.

Remember Mary and Martha? Mary was sitting at the feet of Jesus, listening to him talk. So Martha complained because Mary wasn't helping her prepare dinner. "But the Lord said to her, 'Martha, dear friend, you are so upset over all these details! There is really only one thing worth being concerned about. Mary has discovered it—and I won't take it away from her!' " (Luke 10:41,42 TLB).

This passage emphasizes that God wants our love and devotion first and foremost. He is not primarily concerned about what we do for Him, how hard we work for Him, or how noble our service is; His primary concern is that we love Him.

In James 2:8, the second greatest commandment—loving your neighbor as yourself—is referred to as the "royal law," implying that it is of foremost significance. Let me comment briefly on this command, for it is an important one and a misunderstood one.

There are some people who have never learned to accept themselves or love themselves. It is then very difficult, if not impossible, for them to genuinely love other people. Often in the past we've gotten this backward. We've been told to love God first, our neighbor second, and ourself third. For awhile there was even a bumper sticker and a lapel pin that said "I am Third."

I don't believe this is what the Bible teaches. Yes, we are to love God first, but then we are to love ourselves and our neighbors equally.

People who are wrestling with many emotional difficulties, working on their own relationship with God and their own self-esteem, may need to emphasize loving themselves as well as others.

AVOID UNNECESSARY RULES

The next thing to do in order to avoid guilt is to avoid unnecessary rules. I've frequently heard ministers who were preaching against cults quote Revelation 22:18, which says not to add to or take away from the Scriptures. But I've yet to hear it said from the pulpit that when we add the do's and the don't's of legalistic Christian living, perhaps we're also guilty of adding to Scripture. And when we do this we become crippled with bondage and false guilt (see Deuteronomy 12:32).

I've discovered that it's a full-time job obeying the commands that God clearly asks me to keep. So I decided a few years ago that I would work on the things that are clearly enumerated in the Bible, and not worry about those that weren't so clear.

BE CAREFUL OF COMMITMENTS

Hastily made commitments can create a great deal of guilt, because every time we make a promise and fail to keep it, we're guilty—and this time it's *true* guilt.

The children of Israel learned a bitter lesson

about making commitments when they hastily made a contract with the neighboring nation of Gibeon, without consulting God. The Gibeonites were afraid of the Israelites because they had heard how God had helped them conquer other nations in their march across the Promised Land, so they tricked the Israelites into making a peace treaty with them.

Several days later the Israelites realized they had been deceived, but they were still bound to their oath: "We have sworn to them by the Lord, the God of Israel, and now we cannot touch them" (Joshua 9:19). They were bound by their commitment.

In Ecclesiastes 5:4,5 we read this warning: "When you make a vow to God, do not be late in paying it.... It is better that you should not vow than that you should vow and not pay."

Another item that falls under the category of commitments is assuming leadership in the church or in your profession. Those assuming any leadership should consider the gravity of their position. James 3:1 says, "Let not many of you become teachers, my brethren, knowing that as such we shall incur a stricter judgment." When we take on these additional roles, we are held responsible for them, and so we should take them on only after giving the matter much thought and prayer. If we take on commitments and are unable to fulfill them, we violate valid "shoulds," and thus are subject to valid guilt.

ERASE OLD TAPES

During our formative years, we pick up numerous messages from the important people around us. These are recorded on our mental tape recorder, which is constantly filing away all the messages sent our way, whether we believe them or not, whether they are true or not. The process starts immediately after birth, and to some extent continues throughout our life. Many tapes are patently false messages that greatly complicate our lives. Here is a list of some of the more common tapes. Note that the messages may remain in their original form as "You're stupid," or may be internalized as "I'm stupid." Either form is equally destructive.

You're no good.
You're a brat.
You're stupid.
You're dumb.
You're ugly.
You're good for nothing.
You're so lazy.
You're such a slob.
You're so irresponsible.
You never carry through on things.
You're so selfish.
I can never do anything right.
I'll never amount to anything.
I have to please everybody.
Everybody should like me.
I don't deserve anything better.

Look what I did now.
I better not get my hopes up—something
bad always happens.

These are just a few of the more common
tapes that play in people's minds. I would urge
you to think about what your tapes are and how
they tend to influence you. You may even want
to write them down. You may also want to list
the origin—whether it was your mother, father,
or teacher who said it. It might also help to
note the incidents in your life that reinforced
the message. Then whenever you are influenced
by one of those tapes, identify that a tape is
playing.

The next step is to actively counter that
negative message with a positive one. For example, if the message has been "You dummy,
you'll never amount to anything," the new tape
might be the familiar saying, "But God doesn't
make junk!"

A great deal of reprogramming must be done
to counteract these tapes. Every time the old
destructive tape emerges, identify it as such, remind yourself that it is untrue, and play the correct tape instead. This takes some work, and
changes will not take place overnight, but with
patience and persistence the cruel messages that
were picked up during your formative years can
be erased.

WHEN TO GET COUNSEL

If a pilot who doesn't know how to fly by

instruments flies through solid clouds or a storm, he won't be able to stay on course because he doesn't have the horizon on which to focus. Inevitably he will go to the right or to the left a little, up a little or down a little. It doesn't matter which way he goes—the end result is catastrophic.

I once heard a tape recording of a pilot in this very predicament. He had no instruments, and as he realized he was steadily going off course, you could hear the panic in his voice. He knew he was in trouble, but he didn't know which way to turn. No matter which direction he turned, it didn't seem right, and as his voice rose in desperation, you could picture him struggling with the controls. Then all of a sudden—nothing. The plane had crashed.

People who get into deep trouble with guilt or depression are often like that pilot without instruments. What they need is outside help in order to regain their equilibrium. Otherwise they can get into a tailspin, with devastating results.

God has made man so that at times he needs to seek help from other people. And for some people, particularly men, this is a very difficult thing to do; however, sometimes it is God's chosen means of deliverance.

Think of the apostle Paul, for example. Paul was a strong, powerful person. Yet he was a guilty man who was trying to please God in his own way. When God stopped him in his tracks on the way to Damascus, he was stricken with blindness. What was the message that God sent to him? It was to go to Ananias, who would pray for God to restore his sight (Acts 9). Paul had to ask someone else, one of those Christians he had been persecuting, to help him.

Naaman, captain of the Syrian army, was called a "great man," a "highly respected" man, and a "valiant warrior" (2 Kings 5:1 ff.). However, he was afflicted by leprosy. He went to Elisha for healing, who told him he would be cleansed of his leprosy if he would wash in the muddy Jordan River.

This was repulsive to Naaman and made him furious. He couldn't understand why he had to bathe in the muddy river when there were rivers in Syria that were sparkling clear. He probably felt humiliated, but his servants encouraged him to give the prophet's advice a try—after all, he didn't have anything to lose. So he did, and was healed.

Not only is it difficult to humble ourselves to seek help, but it's also difficult for some of us to accept the advice of other people who may be older and wiser, or even younger and wiser. We have to be willing to do whatever God wants. I can remember a number of times in my life when I finally had to say, "Lord, I'll do whatever You want." If we don't do this—if we balk—we may be rejecting God's means of deliverance.

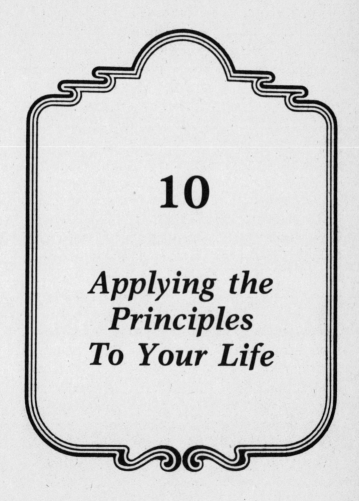

10

Applying the Principles To Your Life

JOAN AND MARY

Joan was flying back from visiting with her family in Chicago, and had asked her friend Mary to pick her up at the airport on Tuesday morning at 10 A.M. Mary had agreed.

So on Tuesday at 9:30 A.M. Mary left for the airport, since it usually takes a half-hour to get there. However, she forgot about all the construction going on at the airport, so she arrived about 10 minutes late.

When she drove up to the curb, Joan looked very disgusted. Mary apologized profusely for being late, but Joan's only response was to complain about having to wait among the construction with all its dust and dirt. Joan proceeded to tell her friend that she should have known better—"After all, the construction has been going on for a year!" She started coughing, and the two rode home in silence except for an occasional cough from Joan.

Despite her many apologies, Mary felt that Joan was still very angry with her. So after she dropped her off, Mary still felt miserable. Then she spotted a candy store, and, knowing that Joan liked chocolates, Mary stopped and bought a pound of candy. Then she drove back to Joan's house to deliver her gift. In spite of Joan's somewhat curt "Thank you," Mary drove home feeling a little better.

Why don't you try putting down the book at this point to think about the interaction between Joan and Mary. Were there guilt feelings? If so, how were they manifested? Was it true or false guilt? Was Mary led by her feelings? How could she have handled this situation more constructively?

THE ANALYSIS

Since Mary had agreed to pick up Joan and was late, there was some true guilt involved. She did leave on time, however, and simply forgot about the construction. In addition, Joan inflicted some classic guilt trips of the *Laying on the Guilt* and *Shame on You* varieties. A large part of their interaction was through body language alone, which was in fact very effective—Joan's coughing and silence.

Mary was led by her guilt feelings and tried to get rid of her discomfort by buying the candy. She probably did "feel" better after delivering the gift; however, she also fed into the destructive interaction between herself and Joan.

How might Mary have handled this situation? She could have worked harder to arrive on time. But let's assume she "blew it"; then how could she have handled this most constructively?

Certainly, one sincere apology was in order: "Joan, I'm sorry I'm late. I totally forgot about the construction at the airport. Please forgive me." A mature person would accept this, and the relationship would go on without any alienation.

However, the apology wasn't accepted, as evidenced by Joan's coughing and aloofness. A confrontive "I feel" message would be in order (this is discussed in my book *Overcoming Hurts and Anger*). Mary might say, "Joan, ever since you got in the car, I've had the feeling that you're upset with me. Are you still angry that I was late?" Hopefully this would open the lines of verbal communication so that there can be resolution of the problem. Regardless of whether they are able to work through the situation, Mary should not yield to her false guilt feeling by buying the chocolates.

Let's see if we can clarify the process of working through guilt feelings. When we feel guilty, the first step is to try to determine what is causing the feeling and whether it represents true or false guilt. Now let's look a little further at the process of evaluating false guilt. *Labeling* the process helps. For example, when I was in Gemco and realized that my uncomfortable feeling stemmed from the "tyranny of the shoulds'" and an old tape, it helped me diffuse the guilt feelings.

In the problem between Mary and Joan, it would have been helpful for Mary to realize that Joan was laying guilt trips on her, and to label which ones they were.

Another example of labeling is clearly identifying a false accusation. When you do this, it's much easier to see the situation for exactly what it is, and thus be able to resist it. This is what Jesus did when He rebuked Peter's false statement in Matthew 16:21-23, and what Job did when his friends were slinging false accusations at him.

Countering old tapes, guilt trips, or false accusations with the truth also helps you deal with them. Reminding myself that I'm not lazy when I relax on a Friday afternoon, that I don't have to work all the time, and that rest and relaxation are appropriate, helps negate the false guilt. Jesus certainly did this when He rebutted Satan's accusation with Scripture in Matthew 4:7.

Let's try to apply these principles with another example.

MIKE AND PETE

Mike is 20; his wife, Cheryl, is 19. They have two children in diapers. They occasionally attend church, where they met Pete. Pete is a conscientious Christian, and since Mike didn't have a job, Pete hunted around his company and drummed up a job for him.

And since Mike's car wasn't running, Pete offered to pick him up. So he did this the first day, and the second, but three months went by and he still drove a couple of miles out of his way every day to take Mike to and from work.

Soon it came time for Pete's vacation. Two weeks in advance he told Mike he would be leaving and wouldn't be able to take him to work, and asked Mike if he might have his car running by then. Mike's reply was that he didn't really know, and that he would have a hard time getting to work without a ride. Pete suggested that he check a bus schedule, but Mike didn't seem very interested in that option either.

Then out of the blue Mike asked, "You're flying to Hawaii for your vacation, aren't you?" The implication was obvious—Mike thought Pete should loan him his car. By this time Pete was feeling very uncomfortable, so he said he would talk to Bill in the front office, who might be able to drive Mike to work.

This relieved Pete of some of the tension he was feeling. But the days slipped by, and Pete felt a little awkward about approaching Bill, but he also felt awkward about talking to Mike again. He didn't want to loan Mike his car because it was a new car, and Mike didn't take very good care of things. That decision caused Pete a great deal of turmoil because he thought, "A good Christian would loan it to him—I'm being selfish; I'm placing too much value on material things."

So because he was busy getting ready for vacation, he ended up not loaning the car to Mike and not talking to Bill about giving Mike a ride.

This put a damper on his vacation because he felt a little guilty. Then as soon as he walked into church after his vacation, he was greeted with, "Have you seen Mike and Cheryl? I heard Mike lost his job!"

With that, Pete's heart sank. As soon as he got out of church, he rushed home to call Mike. Mike was gone, and Cheryl said that because Pete didn't talk to Bill, Mike didn't have a way to get to work and was laid off. He started drinking again, Cheryl went on to say, and they had very little money, and their rent was due . . . . So Pete said he would see what he could do. He hung up the phone feeling horrible, and even wondered whether he should draw some money out of his bank account to help his friends.

Now what is your evaluation of this? Pete did say that he would talk to Bill, but he didn't, so does that constitute true guilt? Is he responsible for the fact that Mike lost his job and went back to drinking?

THE ANALYSIS

Pete is to be commended for going out of his way for Mike by getting the job for him and driving him to and from work for three months. However, conscientious individuals like this often take on responsibilities that rightfully belong to other people. When Mike made an overture to use Pete's new car, it started an old tape of Pete's: "I'm being selfish." To label that tape and to remember how his dad used to tell him "You're so selfish" would have helped Pete understand his reaction to Mike's manipulation. He could then counter it with the fact that he really does give of himself to other people and this might help ease his false guilt.

However, since he did promise to talk to Bill, he should have followed through on his commitment. Not doing so led to some true guilt. An apology for this would be in order.

But most of the responsibility rightfully belongs to Mike. When Mike said that he would have a hard time getting to work without a ride or a car, Pete could have labeled it as an *It Will Be Your Fault* guilt trip. This might have helped Pete communicate to Mike that he was capable of finding a way to work *if* he chose to do so.

Cheryl also employed the *It Will Be Your Fault* guilt trip when she said, "Mike didn't have a way to work" and "You didn't talk to Bill." If Pete were able to identify this it would help him feel less guilty. It would also help him to be less defensive with Cheryl.

Should Pete keep helping Mike? This is an extremely difficult question, one which goes beyond the scope of our subject. Suffice it to say that Pete must weigh Mike's need for help with his need to learn to help himself.

ELAINE

Elaine is a 26-year-old mother of three. She is a Christian, and is trying to live the Christian life. Her mother called her on the phone one day and said, "Elaine, it's your birthday, and I've decided to have your birthday dinner Saturday night. I have invited your uncle and aunt, and they have the evening available. I will expect you and the family at 6 P.M. sharp."

Elaine replied, trying to stall her, "Uh—I'm not sure about Ned's schedule. I don't know what his plans are for that night."

Mother smoothly replied, "Oh, I'm sure you can work that out. I know he doesn't like to come over very much—some Christian he is. Doesn't the Bible say something about honoring your parents? I think that should apply to your in-laws, too."

Mother continued to talk and dominate the conversation for another ten minutes, and then finally she said, "See you Saturday, dearie," and hung up.

Elaine got off the phone feeling upset and confused. She thought to herself, "We should go. Mother does mean well. After all, she isn't a Christian, and we want to influence her for Christ. She goes to a lot of work for these dinners."

But then she thought of the other side, "Ned

just hates to go there, and the kids are even starting to complain. They dislike the way mom orders them around.''

Then Elaine thought wishfully, ''Maybe my sore throat will turn into the flu. Or maybe I'll get pneumonia, and I won't have to go.''

Then she remembered that this was exactly the type of thing that made Ned threaten divorce a year earlier.

She was still mulling this over in her mind three days later, when her sister from Northern California called. ''Oh, I heard mom's having your birthday dinner Saturday night— you *are* going to go, aren't you?'' she said. Elaine replied that she wasn't quite sure, to which her sister replied, ''You know, you'd better consider mom's eternal future,'' because both sisters are Christians and their mother is not.

Given the situation, Elaine's most promising option seems to be catching pneumonia.

The background to this quandary is that as far back as Elaine can remember, if she failed to do something her mother wanted, her mother would say things like, ''You self-centered, spoiled child. You always want things your own way. You never think of anyone else. You always think about what you want. You're selfish. You don't appreciate all that I do for you.'' But in reality Elaine is a very sensitive, giving, conscientious person.

Elaine had a very formative experience when

she was about seven. Her mother wanted her to take piano lessons very badly, but Elaine wanted to learn to play the flute. They had a little tug-of-war over it, and it was the one time that Elaine stood up to her mother and said no. She really wanted flute lessons. Her mother told her she was being selfish, and then said, "You're making me have chest pains." For three days she stayed in bed, complaining of her chest pains and telling poor Elaine, "something like this could kill a person."

Since then Elaine has never spoken up for herself, especially around her mother.

Also, Elaine never got a compliment during her childhood, in spite of the fact that she had almost straight A's in school. Her mother felt that praise would go to a child's head.

THE ANALYSIS

Let me try to illustrate what is happening to Elaine on the opposite page.

Here's poor Elaine, the figure with the sad face, and her tapes are hounding her with "If you don't go, you're selfish. You need to please everyone. You're a spoiled brat if you don't go."

She's getting pressure from her mother, husband, children, and sister. Elaine feels in a box, in a no-win situation. If she obeys her mother, she won't be obeying her husband, and if she obeys her husband, she won't be obeying her mother.

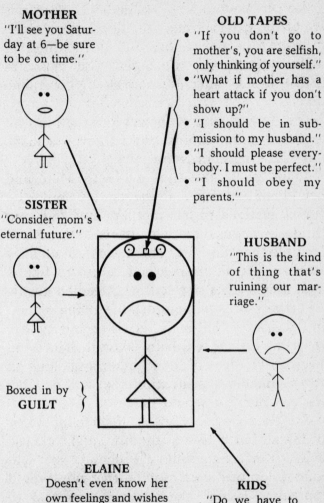

MOTHER
"I'll see you Saturday at 6—be sure to be on time."

OLD TAPES
- "If you don't go to mother's, you are selfish, only thinking of yourself."
- "What if mother has a heart attack if you don't show up?"
- "I should be in submission to my husband."
- "I should please everybody. I must be perfect."
- "I should obey my parents."

SISTER
"Consider mom's eternal future."

HUSBAND
"This is the kind of thing that's ruining our marriage."

Boxed in by **GUILT**

ELAINE
Doesn't even know her own feelings and wishes about her birthday, to say nothing about having her wishes met.

KIDS
"Do we have to go? We hate it at grandma's."

But the most devastating thing in all of this is not the external manipulation and pressure from the people involved, but the internal pressure from the old tapes. The messages in the tapes alone are a mass of contradictions.

This is the kind of boxed-in situation that leads people into confusion, guilt, psychosomatic illnesses, and depression.

Again, as in the situtaion with Mike and Pete, Elaine must weigh the valid "shoulds"— her obligations to her mother, husband, and children versus her own needs and wishes. To help her do this, she needs to identify the inappropriate tapes and refuse to follow their edicts. This step will help tremendously.

Furthermore, pinpointing the manipulation and guilt trips that both her sister and mother are using on her will help. Then if Elaine and Ned can get their heads together and agree on how to handle this situation, that will be a big load off Elaine's shoulders.

This time they may choose to go to mother's; or Elaine, with Ned's support, might choose to confront her mother. Probably she will want to inform her mother that she would appreciate being asked rather than told to come to her own birthday dinner. At some point she may want to inform her sister of her concern for her mother's "eternal future," but that is a separate issue from the birthday party.

By God's help, by applying the principles

discussed in this book, and by Ned's support Elaine can make significant progress in getting out of the horrible box in which she finds herself.

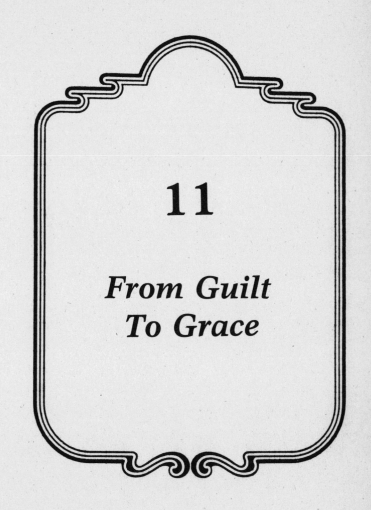

11

From Guilt To Grace

*I*n the preceding chapter we have focused primarily on what we can do to resolve shame and guilt, the problem plaguing mankind. Yet without God all our efforts would be in vain. Apart from God's grace, we are truly guilty. It is only because of His love that we are declared "not guilty." While what we have discussed previously is important, far surpassing this is what Christ has done for us to remove our shame and guilt. He has cleansed, justified, freed, and forgiven us, and He deeply loves us. All this is available to all who accept Christ as Savior.

The book of Ephesians overflows with descriptions of God's grace. It says that we are blessed, we are covered with His love, we are showered with the riches of His grace. Paul says in his prayer for the Christians in Ephesus, "I pray for you constantly, asking God, the glorious Father of our Lord Jesus Christ, to give you wisdom to see clearly and really understand who Christ is and all that he has done for you. I pray that your hearts will be flooded with light so that you can see something of the future he has called you to share. I want you to realize that God has been made rich because we who are Christ's have been given to him! I pray that you will begin to understand how incredibly great his power is to help those who believe him'' (Ephesians 1:16-19 TLB).

The overwhelming message is that God has lavishly showered His love upon us. Not only does He love us and delight in us, but He continues to forgive and forget our sin, earnestly desiring that we live a life free of guilt.

In Jeremiah 31:34 the Lord declares, ''I will forgive their iniquity, and their sin I will remember no more.'' In Isaiah 38:17 we read, ''For Thou has cast all my sins behind Thy back.'' God is saying unequivocally that He forgives us and will forget our sin, that He even puts it behind His back, never to be held against us.

Psalm 103:11,12 puts it this way: ''For as high as the heavens are above the earth, so great is His lovingkindness toward those who fear Him. As far as the east is from the west''—a whole world apart—''so far has He removed our transgressions from us.'' Hebrews 10:17 says, ''Their sins and their lawless deeds I will remember no more.'' Then there is the ringing declaration of Romans 8:1: ''There is therefore now no condemnation for those who are in Christ Jesus.''

God's grace and forgiveness are continuous. Continuous means ''prolonged, without interruption, unbroken.'' His forgiveness is not only for the sins of the past, but it will continue throughout our lives.

I believe that God's forgiveness continues even when we aren't aware of any sin. However, when we are aware of the fact that we have sinned, then God wants us to admit that sin to Him, primarily because it restores how we feel about our relationship with God and helps resolve our internal conflicts and our relations with other people, nipping in the bud any emotional complications.

God paid the price for sin on the cross once and for all, and we are forgiven once and for all. First John 1:7 says, "But if we walk in the light as He Himself is in the light, we have fellowship with one another, and the blood of Jesus his Son cleanses us from all sin." The word "cleansing" here is referring to God's continuous action— He keeps on cleansing us.

God has promised not only to count us free from the sins of the past and present, but He has promised to continue right up to the day that we see Him face-to-face. First Corinthians 1:8,9 emphasizes our guiltless position before God, saying that God "guarantees right up to the end that you will be counted free from all sin and guilt on that day when he returns. God will surely do this for you, for he always does just what he says, and he is the one who invited you into this wonderful friendship with his Son, even Christ our Lord" (TLB).

What else is God offering along with His forgiveness? He offers us freedom, and urges us to hold fast to that freedom. Galatians 5:1 says, "It was for freedom that Christ set us free;

therefore keep standing firm and do not be subject again to the yoke of slavery."

It's so easy for us to slip into a life characterized by works-oriented grace, attempting to ease our guilt by working zealously, trying harder and harder to be better Christians and falling into a life of bondage rather than freedom.

What happens to so many Christians is that they get entangled in a lot of shoulds, oughts, and musts. Often when a person first becomes a Christian he is walking on clouds, and Christianity is the greatest thing in the world. But when you see him three, five, or seven years down the road he is weighed down with guilt, or he feels that he must somehow earn God's love. Somewhere he has lost his sense of God's love. So he begins to feel that if he witnesses more, tithes more, and works at the church seven nights a week—it's never put that way, but that's how it's lived out—then he will continue in God's grace.

This is precisely the problem Paul was addressing when he wrote to the Galatians, "I am amazed that you are so quickly deserting Him who called you by the grace of Christ, for a different gospel.... Having begun by the Spirit, are you now being perfected by the flesh?... For as many as are of the works of the Law are under a curse; for it is written, 'Cursed is everyone who does not abide by all things written in the book of the Law, to perform them' " (Galatians 1:6; 3:3,10).

If our salvation is based on our performance, then we have to carry that to its logical conclusion and keep every single command. We'll never make it that way, and so the message is, "Don't even try."

Remember the story of the king who was catching up with the people who owed him money, and he summoned a slave who owed him about 20 million dollars (Matthew 18:23-30)? The debtor fell at the feet of the king and begged to be given some time, pleading that he not be thrown into prison. Those were exactly the words used in the original Greek manuscript—that the man wanted time to repay. He didn't ask for forgiveness; he asked the king for time to pay his debt.

Do you know how the king responded? He released and forgave him. But the slave still had it in his head that he had to pay back the debt. So he found a man who owed him about 20 dollars—a pittance in comparison with the millions he owed the king—and demanded immediate payment. The man couldn't pay, so he threw him into debtors' prison.

That's often what we do. When we don't sense God's full forgivenesss, when we don't realize that we're totally released, we can't forgive ourselves and are harsh with other people. We're like the man who was frantically trying to pay off his multimillion-dollar debt, which is something we'll never be able to do.

The message is not that you have ten more

years to work for Christ and then you'll measure up. It's that every one of us who has accepted Christ is already released—already forgiven. The penalty has been paid, and as we come to realize God's love and limitless forgiveness, it helps us to be more forgiving toward both ourselves and other people.

Let's look at a few more verses on grace. Romans 9:16 says, "So then it does not depend on the man who wills or the man who runs, but on God who has mercy." God's grace does not depend on our human effort. Colossians 2:14 says that God has "canceled out the certificate of debt consisting of decrees against us and which was hostile to us; and He has taken it out of the way, having nailed it to the cross."

Hebrews 10:18 says, "Now where there is forgiveness of these things, there is no longer any offering for sin." This is the message of grace— that we stop working for our acceptance. God's grace, as we grasp hold of it, is the solution to all guilt.

The Greek word for grace is *charis,* which means gracefulness, graciousness, kindness, or favor. In the New Testament it has further connotations of undeserved, unmerited, freely given favor.

The result of grace is *joy,* a word that literally comes from the root word "grace." Nehemiah 8 illustrates the joy that springs from God's grace. The priests were reading the law to the people, who hadn't heard it because they had been in captivity for years. As they listened, the people wept and mourned and grieved; they were truly contrite for their sins.

Then God spoke to them through a prophet, saying, " 'This day is holy to the Lord your God; do not mourn or weep.' For all the people were weeping when they heard the words of the law. Then he said to them, 'Go, eat of the fat, drink of the sweet, and send portions to him who has nothing prepared; for this day is holy to our Lord. Do not be grieved, for the joy of the Lord is your strength' " (Nehemiah 8:9,10).

This is the gospel, even in these few Old Testament verses. God uses guilt to bring us to Him. But He doesn't leave us there laboring under our guilt. He lifts us up and sets us next to Himself. And His message to us, like His message to the Israelites, is simply to rejoice, to celebrate, to "eat of the fat, drink of the sweet."

God's benediction for us, His message to all of us laboring under the guilt from which He longs so to free us, is contained in Ephesians 3:17: "May your roots go down deep into the soil of God's marvelous love; and may you be able to feel and understand, as all God's children should, how long, how wide, how deep, and how high his love really is; and to experience this love for yourselves" (TLB).

Psalm 32:1,2 TLB says, "What happiness for those whose guilt has been forgiven! What

166 / FROM GUILT TO GRACE

joys when sins are covered over! What relief for those who have confessed their sins and God has cleared their record!"

My prayer is that you may comprehend God's love and grace toward you, and rejoice in your guiltless position before Him.

RECOMMENDED READING

Carlson, Dwight L, M.D. *How to Win Over Fatigue.* Old Tappan, New Jersey: Fleming H. Revell, 1974.

Carlson, Dwight L., M.D. *Overcoming Hurts and Anger.* Eugene, Oregon: Harvest House, 1981.

Cooke, Joseph R. *Free for the Taking.* Old Tappan, New Jersey: Fleming H. Revell, 1975.

Hummel, Charles E. *Tyranny of the Urgent.* Downers Grove, Illinois: InterVarsity, 1967.

Justice, William G.R. *Guilt and Forgiveness.* Grand Rapids: Baker, 1980.

Phillips, J.B. *Your God Is Too Small.* New York: Macmillan, 1957.

Tournier, Paul, M.D. *Guilt and Grace.* New York: Harper & Row, 1958.

NOTES

NOTES

NOTES